Salads
&
Salad
Dressings

Salads & Salad Dressings

FOR
FOODSERVICE
MENU
PLANNING

Selected

by

EULALIA C. BLAIR

Jule Wilkinson, Editor

Published by
INSTITUTIONS/VOLUME FEEDING MAGAZINE

Distributed by Cahners Books, 89 Franklin Street, Boston, Massachusetts 02110

Library of Congress Catalog Card No. 73-89528
ISBN 0-8436-0576-6

Printed in the United States of America

TABLE OF CONTENTS

ACKNOWLEDGEMENTS

It is very nice to be able to express my grateful thanks and sincere appreciation to the many talented technicians who have given of their thinking, time and skill to initiate the recipes collected in this book. And to my business and professional associates with food processors, manufacturers, public relations firms, advertising agencies, associations and institutions who so generously supplied recipe material for *Volume Feeding Management Magazine* during the years when it was a separate magazine. And who now have answered my call again and furnished the photographs for this book.

I am also glad of this opportunity to say "Thank You" to the warmhearted foodservice operators who, again and again, shared favorite recipes from their kitchens.

And to add a very special thank-you to Mrs. Jule Wilkinson for her excellent counsel and capable help in designing, editing and taking care of the endless details concerned with publishing this book.

Eulalia C. Blair

INTRODUCTION

IT WAS WITH pleasure and pride that I put together the recipes that make up this book. I hope that you will find equal pleasure and satisfaction as you put them to use.

I don't know when the art of salad making first captured my attention but it has provoked my interest and challenged my talents for most of my life. While I thoroughly enjoy cooking of every kind, it is salad making that gives me the greatest delight. I learned from my mother, from teachers and from a dozen or more capable salad girls. And I also learned a great deal more while supervising salad rooms and cafeteria counters and watching attractive salads as they sold.

Believing that a picture is worth more than words, once— on finding that a particular salad was hard to describe—I made up the salad to show the president of the company I was working for (a cafeteria chain devoted to noontime meals). He liked what he saw and, to my surprise, promptly gave me the assignment to standardize salad recipes for the entire chain. The project was my pet—an enjoyable job from beginning to end.

I still believe in the picture theory and have included a number of photographs to illustrate this book. I am also passing along my treasury of salad making tips gathered from here and there over the years.

Trends in salad making have changed during the length of time I've had to observe them. First, as is obvious, today's markets give us more salad materials to work with than in yesteryear. And these ingredients are now made available every month of the year.

The time-honored slaws and gelatins continue to maintain their well-earned following. Main-dish salads have become far more varied and increasingly popular as offerings at lunchtime and on the buffet. But the fussy salads like the "candlestick," and similar concoctions designed to represent an object other than food, came into favor some years ago and then (and quite happily) went out of vogue.

There's now greater emphasis on simple green salads and salad bowls with attention to dressings and their supporting

A Classic Salad Presentation

Western Growers Assn.

role. Many food service operators are taking advantage of the showmanship that preparation at tableside affords. And others recognize the patron-pleasing potential of an inviting salad bar.

This book includes recipes for a broad range of salads and salad dressings together with charts, merchandising suggestions and other guidelines. With it comes my sincere wish that the recipes and text will provide inspiration and a helping hand to bring your salad making newfound measures of success.

SALADS

The Classics and Other Members of the Clan

THE VERY EARLIEST salads were little more than tender leaves. And to this day the classic salad is still the noble green. It consists of tastefully dressed leaves and nothing else—save possibly a garnish.

These green salads are of two types. One is the tossed variety (a mixture of torn leaves). The other is the arranged green salad, made with items such as a wedge of lettuce, a heart of romaine or a bouquet of cress that keeps its identity and shape and makes a salad in itself.

By the strictest definition, these are the true salads. But, in practice, the salad picture is a much broader one than that. The term "salad," as it is used today, includes a vast assortment of cooked and uncooked foods, prepared or served with dressing, and arranged on leafy greens. The ingredients take into account a wide variety of vegetables and fruits as well as heartier items such as cold meats, fish, seafood, eggs and cheese.

All types of salads can occupy a lively niche within the salad scheme. For the sophisticated menu there's nothing that rivals the grace of the elegantly simple salad based on cool, crisp, crunchy greens. But it is quite in order to list salads of the fussier sort with a casual meal.   And to feature robust salads—those filled with meats and cheese—as a main dish item on the noontime menu.   Also, it's well known among menu makers that many of these hearty salad mixtures are excellent choices to set off a cold buffet.

Variety in greens is one of the basic secrets of tossed salads.   But **quality** *is even more telling.   For the success of every salad, regardless of type, depends upon the freshness, crispness and perky good looks of the greens.*

As for the guidelines, the selection of the salad greens is extremely important.   And, essential, too, is conscientious handling of the perishable greens.   This should begin the moment they are received.   Adhering to the rules, prompt refrigeration, adequate washing, efficient draining, and thorough chilling are the crucial points to observe.   Withal, you can never overrate the vital importance of leaves that are clean, dry, delightfully cold and brittle-crisp.

Salad Set for Spicy Tossing

American Spice Trade Assn.

GREEN SALADS

Tossed Salads

THERE are unlimited possibilities for varying the tossed green salads. In themselves, the leafy greens offer a profusion of textures, flavors, and shapes. Moreover, they add a color range that extends from nearly-white to the deepest shade of green.

The major source of salad material is the lettuce clan. It includes crisphead or iceberg; the butterhead, which takes in Boston and Bibb (sometimes called limestone); leaf lettuce (the kind that doesn't head); and cos lettuce (or romaine).

There's also escarole, curly endive (or "chicory"), the bleached chicory which goes by the name of Belgian or French or Witloof endive, and watercress. Spinach, celery leaves, anise (fennel or finochio), and the plant called arugula, which is sometimes available in Italian markets, supply other kinds of foliage. These can often be used to advantage to give a tossed green salad a distinctive touch.

With the market offering such a diversity of choices, you can create dozens of attractive combinations by merely maneuvering with greens. To further indicate the potential, each of these salads, in turn, readily accepts an endless variety of trimmings, either as an added ingredient or as a garnish for the top.

And besides all these, there's the wondrous array of dressings which can vary every one of them!

The character of the additions you select depends largely on the type of salad you have in mind. For an accompaniment salad, consider marinated sliced uncooked mushrooms, snipped fresh herbs or one of the other salad bowl additions outlined in the list below. Simply toss this "extra" along with the greens.

Salad Bowl Additions

ALMONDS *toasted*
  sliced; shredded
ANCHOVY *filets*
  pieces; whole (garnish only)
APPLE, *red, unpeeled*
  slices; cubes; matchstick pieces
AVOCADO
  slices; cubes; balls
ARTICHOKES, *canned bottoms*
  or cooked frozen hearts,
  marinated
BACON
  crisp bits
BEETS, *pickled*
  slices; julienne strips
BREAD STUFFING MIX
CABBAGE, *red*
  shreds
CAPERS
CAULIFLOWER, *raw*
  slices or flowerlets
CARROTS, *raw*
  curls; shreds; thin slices
CELERY
  slices; diagonal slices; stuffed
  (short lengths)
CHEESE
  Blue or Roquefort
    crumbled
  Cream
    cubes; balls

Cottage
  small scoops (garnish only)
Swiss or American
  cubes; shreds; slivers; strips
Parmesan
  grated (effective garnish on
  dark leaves)
CHIVES, *snipped*
CROUTONS, *toasted*
  plain or seasoned
CUCUMBERS, *peeled or unpeeled*
  scored slices; dice; half or
  quarter slices
EGGS, *hard-cooked*
  slices; quarters; wedges; julienne
  strips; sieved
FISH
  Crabmeat; Lobster; Salmon,
  fresh, canned or smoked;
  Sardines; Scallops (poached
  and chilled); Shrimp; Tuna
GRAPEFRUIT
  sections
GRAPES *Ribier*
  halves (seeded)
HEARTS OF PALM
HERBS, *fresh*
  snipped
  (add dry herbs with dressing)

MEAT
*Chicken; Ham; Luncheon
Meats; Roast Beef, rare;
Turkey strips, julienne cuts*
MONOSODIUM GLUTAMATE
all-purpose or with flavor
MUSHROOMS
*marinated raw slices
small whole pickled
mushrooms*
OLIVES
Green
whole (garnish only)
Ripe
*whole (garnish only;)
pieces*
Stuffed
whole; slices
ONIONS, *sweet or red
very thin slices*
ORANGES
sections; quarter slices
PARSLEY
*chopped; sprigs (garnish
only)*
PIMIENTO, *canned
strips*

PINEAPPLE, *fresh, frozen or
canned chunks; tidbits*
POMEGRANATE SEEDS
POTATO OR CORN CHIPS
coarsely broken bits
RADISHES
slices; roses (for garnish)
SCALLIONS, *snipped*
SESAME SEEDS, *toasted*
TANGERINES
sections; dice
TOMATOES
*wedges; quarter slices
whole or halves of cherry tomatoes
slices of yellow tomatoes
(garnish)*
VEGETABLES, *cooked, marinated
Asparagus tips; Broccoli flowerlets; Green Beans; Carrot Strips;
Cauliflower flowerlets*
WALNUTS, *halves, toasted
plain or seasoned*
WATER CHESTNUTS
sliced
ZUCCHINI, *raw
thin slices*

Fresh Vegetables Vary a Tossed Salad

Western Growers Assn.

Heartier Ingredients for Salad Bowl

Western Growers Assn.

Heartier Salad Bowls

TO CREATE heartier versions of the tossed green salad (the kind that practically makes a meal), you can add a comely combination of fixings—meat, eggs, cheese, and such—treating them as ingredients to mingle with the greens.

Or, you can adopt a completely different idea and plan salads to present in individual bowls. For these, first fill the bowl with greens (tossed with your choice of dressing), then arrange the trimmings in an attractive fashion to decorate the top. As a starting point, try the following combinations using them either to toss with your mixture of greens or as a garnish on top of the bowls:

Whole Shrimp, Cucumber Slices, Chopped Parsley and Chives
Marinated Whole Green Beans, Artichoke Hearts, Julienne
    Swiss Cheese, Bacon Bits
Julienne Chicken, Halved Ribier Grapes, Pineapple Chunks,
    Toasted Walnuts
Whole Shrimp, Quartered Egg, Anchovy Fillets, Capers
Asparagus Tips, Strips of Ham and Cheese, Carrot Curls, Ripe
    Olives
Halved Cherry Tomatoes, Crumbled Blue Cheese, Croutons

Roast Beef Strips, Green Pepper Rings, Sliced Red Onions
Lobster Chunks, Sliced Egg, Chopped Fresh Dill, Ripe Olives
Julienne Ham, Chicken, Swiss Cheese.
Julienne Tongue, Sliced Egg, Swiss Cheese, Tomato Wedges
Chicken, Anchovy Pieces, Sliced Toasted Almonds
Grapefruit and Orange Sections, Sliced Avocado—With or Without Pomegranate Seeds
Sardines, Quartered Hard-Cooked Egg, Radish Rose
Julienne Pickled Beets, Sliced Egg, Onion Rings
Grapefruit Sections, Avocado Slices, Whole Shrimp
Sliced Radishes, Sliced Cucumber, Tomato Wedges, Green Pepper Strips, Red Cabbage Shreds, Avocado Slices
Sliced Unpeeled Cucumber, Sliced Radishes, Sliced Celery, Tomato Wedges, American Cheese Cubes
Sliced Egg, Julienne Ham, Green Pepper Strips, Cauliflower Slices
Cherry Tomatoes, Sliced Celery, Marinated Artichoke Hearts

BLUE LAKE GREEN BEANS
GOURMET SALAD BOWL

Yield: 24 portions

Ingredients:

BLUE LAKE GREEN BEANS, whole or French style	1 No. 10 can
HEAD LETTUCE	4 heads
TOMATOES, sliced	16
SWISS or AMERICAN CHEESE, cut julienne	1 pound
HAM, boiled or baked or TURKEY or CHICKEN, cooked cut julienne	1 pound
RIPE OLIVES	24

Procedure

1. Drain green beans. Chill, marinating in French dressing, if desired.
2. Arrange a bed of lettuce (leaves or shredded) in bottom of each salad bowl   Place 3 tomato slices on each salad.
3. Arrange cheese and ham strips and green beans between tomato slices.
4. Place a ripe olive on top of each salad. Serve with mayonnaise, French or Louis dressing.

ALASKA KING CRAB SALAD BOWL

Yield: 12 portions

Ingredients

LETTUCE and ROMAINE, medium-size pieces	3 quarts
CUCUMBERS, peeled, sliced	1 cup
CELERY, finely sliced	2 cups
SCALLIONS, finely sliced	8
ALASKA KING CRAB, bite-size pieces	1 quart
BLACK PEPPER, freshly ground	as needed
OIL and VINEGAR DRESSING, well-seasoned	1½ cups

Procedure

1. Combine greens, cucumber, celery and scallions. Add crab meat.
2. Sprinkle with black pepper.
3. Add well-seasoned oil and vinegar dressing; toss lightly to mix.

CHEF'S SALAD BOWL WITH CHICKEN SALAD

Yield: 1 bowl

Ingredients

LETTUCE, LEAF	to line bowl
CHEF'S TOSSED SALAD MIXTURE	2 cups
FRENCH DRESSING	1 ounce
CHICKEN SALAD*	1 No. 12 scoop
THOUSAND ISLAND DRESSING	1 ounce
TOMATO WEDGES (1/8 tomato)	2
RADISH ROSE	1
RIPE OLIVE	1
PARSLEY	1 sprig

Procedure

1. Line salad bowl with lettuce.

2. Toss mixed salad greens and French dressing together in mixing bowl until greens are coated evenly.

3. Place in salad bowl. Place scoop of chicken salad on top; pour Thousand Island dressing over.

4. Garnish with tomato wedges, radish, ripe olive and parsley.

*CHICKEN SALAD

Yield: 8 portions

Ingredients

CHICKEN MEAT, 1/4-inch dice	1 pound
CELERY, 1/4-inch dice	10 ounces
CELERY SALT	1/2 teaspoon
PIMIENTOES, diced	1/4 cup
SALAD DRESSING	1-1/4 cups

Procedure

1. Toss ingredients together lightly to mix.

Note

Use this mixture for sandwich filling also.

SUNSHINE SALAD BOWL
WITH ORANGE-HONEY DRESSING

Yield: 50 1-cup portions

Ingredients

MIXED SALAD GREENS	2 gallons
GREEN BEANS, diagonal-cut, drained	1 No. 10 can
ORANGE SECTIONS	1 quart
ONION RINGS	2 cups

Procedure

1. Combine ingredients; toss together lightly.
2. Portion into salad bowls. Serve with Orange-Honey dressing.*

*ORANGE-HONEY DRESSING

Yield: 1 quart

Ingredients

SALT	1 tablespoon
SUGAR	1 tablespoon
MUSTARD, DRY	2 teaspoons
PAPRIKA	2 teaspoons
PEPPER, WHITE	1/2 teaspoon
SALAD OIL	2 cups
ORANGE JUICE	1 cup
HONEY	2/3 cup
VINEGAR	1/2 cup

Procedure

1. Combine salt, sugar, mustard, paprika and pepper.
2. Add remaining ingredients; beat until well combined.

RUSSIAN SALAD BOWL

Yield: 1 portion

Ingredients

LETTUCE, shredded	2 ounces
ROAST BEEF, cold, julienne	¾ ounce
TURKEY BREAST, cold sliced, julienne	¾ ounce
BOILED HAM, cold, julienne	¾ ounce
AMERICAN CHEESE, processed, sharp, julienne	¾ ounce
CARROTS, diced fine	1 ounce
SWEET GARDEN PEAS, (frozen) cooked	1½ ounces
EGGS, hard cooked	2 wedges
TOMATO	2 wedges
THOUSAND ISLAND DRESSING	2 ounces

Procedure

1. Place shredded lettuce in china soup plate lined with leaf lettuce.
2. Arrange beef, turkey, ham and cheese clockwise on lettuce.
3. Arrange carrots, peas, egg and tomato between groups of meats and cheese.
4. Serve with Thousand Island dressing.

NEW ORLEANS SALAD BOWL ⟶

Yield: 1 portion

Ingredients

LETTUCE, shredded	2½ ounces
SHRIMP, split	6
CELERY HEARTS, diced	½ ounce
GREEN PEPPERS	½ ounce
EGG, hard cooked	3 slices
TOMATO WEDGES	2
THOUSAND ISLAND DRESSING	2 ounces

CHEF'S SALAD BOWL

Yield: 50 portions

Ingredients

ESCAROLE	2 heads
ICEBERG LETTUCE	4 heads
ROMAINE	3 heads
CHICORY	2 heads
TURKEY	2 pounds
TONGUE	2 pounds
HAM	2 pounds
CHEESE, CHEDDAR	3 pounds
RADISHES	3 bunches
CARROTS	2 pounds
TOMATOES	8 pounds

Procedure

1. Cut crisp salad greens into bite size pieces. Toss to mix.

2. Cut turkey, meats and cheese in julienne.

3. Prepare radish roses and carrot curls. Cut tomatoes into wedges.

4. Serve mixed greens in salad bowls. Arrange julienne meats and cheese over top. Garnish with a radish rose, carrot curl and two tomato wedges.

5. Serve with sour cream dressing.

Procedure

1. Place bed of shredded lettuce in a china soup plate lined with lettuce leaves.

2. Arrange the shrimp attractively on the lettuce.

3. Sprinkle with diced celery, diced green peppers and garnish with slices of hard cooked egg and tomato wedges.

4. Serve with Thousand Island dressing on the side.

Variations on Caesar Salad Service

American Spice Trade Assn.

Associated Blue Lake Canners, Inc.

CAESAR SALAD

Yield: 2 portions

Ingredients

ROMAINE and ICEBERG LETTUCE, bite-size pieces	1-1/2 quarts
PARMESAN CHEESE, grated	2 tablespoons
BLUE CHEESE, crumbled	2 tablespoons
SALAD OIL, lightly flavored with garlic	1/3 cup
WORCESTERSHIRE SAUCE	1 teaspoon
SALT	1/4 teaspoon
PEPPER, BLACK, ground	2 or 3 turns of mill
EGG, coddled*	1 small
LEMON JUICE	2 tablespoons
CROUTONS, garlic flavored, ¾-inch	16
ANCHOVY FILLETS, cut in pieces	2

Procedure

1. Place salad greens in a large bowl. Sprinkle on cheese.

2. Mix salad oil with Worcestershire and salt in a small bowl. Drizzle over greens. Grind pepper over top.

3. Toss until leaves glisten with oil.

4. Break coddled egg onto greens; pour lemon juice over all; toss until specks of egg disappear.

5. Add croutons and anchovy pieces. Toss lightly.

*Place egg in boiling water; remove from heat. Let stand 1 minute.

GREEN SALAD WITH GARLIC CROUTONS

Yield: 48 1-cup portions

Ingredients

GARLIC CLOVES, sliced	4 teaspoons
SALAD OIL	1½ cups
BREAD CUBES, soft, ½-inch	1 gallon (1¼ pounds)
LEAF LETTUCE, SPINACH, CURLY ENDIVE and ROMAINE, torn into pieces	3 gallons (5½ pounds)
SALT	4 teaspoons
PEPPER	1½ teaspoons
PARMESAN CHEESE, grated	1½ cups
BLEU CHEESE, crumbled	¾ cup
EGGS, whole	¾ cup
LEMON JUICE	¾ cup

Procedure

1. Soak garlic in salad oil at least 1 hour before using.
2. Pour 1/3 cup garlic oil over bread cubes in shallow baking pan.
3. Toast cubes in 350°F. oven 15 minutes, stirring occasionally.
4. Mix salad greens. Place in two large bowls.
5. Sprinkle half of salt, pepper, Parmesan and Bleu cheese over each bowl of greens. Drizzle half of remaining garlic oil over each.
6. Beat eggs slightly; combine with lemon juice. Add half to each salad bowl.
7. Toss salads gently. Just before serving, add croutons; toss again.

Note

Volume shrinks rapidly after salad is mixed. 18 quarts reduces to 12 quarts within 10 minutes. Do steps 6 and 7 just before serving salad to insure maximum number of portions.

CHEF'S MAIN COURSE SALAD

Yield: 50 portions, about 1 cup each

Ingredients

LETTUCE, ICEBERG, shredded	3 gallons
WATERCRESS, broken in short lengths	3 cups
CHICORY, ENDIVE or SPINACH, broken in pieces	1 gallon
FRENCH DRESSING	1 quart
TOMATOES, cut in wedges	1 quart
TOPPING*	

Procedure

1. Combine greens; lightly toss with dressing. Add tomatoes, mixing gently. Serve in individual bowls with choice of topping.

TOPPING NO. 1*

SHRIMP	2 cans (2 pounds 6 ounces each) or 4 pounds cooked
ANCHOVY FILLETS	1 cup
CHEESE, SWISS, cut in thin strips	10 ounces

TOPPING NO. 2*

AVOCADOS, sliced	8
SALMON or TUNA, CANNED	4 pounds
ARTICHOKE HEARTS	1 quart
CHEESE, BLUE, crumbled	2 cups

TOPPING NO. 3*

TONGUE, HAM or CORNED BEEF, cut in strips	2 pounds
CHICKEN or TURKEY, cut in strips	2 pounds
CHEESE, SWISS, cubed	10 ounces

CHEF'S SALAD

Yield: 16 portions

Ingredients

MIXED GREENS (escarole, chicory, lettuce and romaine)	1 gallon
CELERY, diced	2 cups
HAM, cooked, cut julienne	1 cup
SWISS CHEESE, cut julienne	1 cup
EGGS, hard cooked, sliced	4
PARSLEY, finely chopped	¼ cup
TOMATOES, cut in wedges	8
FRENCH DRESSING, PLAIN or GARLIC	1½ cups

Procedure

1. Chill all ingredients thoroughly.
2. Tear greens into small pieces; toss with celery, ham, cheese, eggs, parsley and tomatoes.
3. Just before serving, add dressing; toss again.

CHEF'S SALAD WITH DRIED BEEF

Yield: 48 portions

Ingredients

LETTUCE	8 heads
DRIED BEEF, thinly sliced, cut in strips	2 pounds
HARD-COOKED EGGS, sliced	24
SWISS CHEESE, julienne	3 pounds
TOMATO WEDGES	8 pounds
CUCUMBERS, sliced	2 quarts
RADISHES, sliced	1½ quarts
GREEN PEPPER RINGS	48
WATERCRESS	4 bunches
VINAIGRETTE DRESSING	as needed

Procedure

1. Tear dry, crisp lettuce into bite-size pieces. Place in salad bowls.
2. Arrange dried beef, sliced eggs, Swiss cheese, tomato wedges, sliced cucumbers and radishes on top.
3. Garnish each portion with green pepper ring and watercress.
4. Serve with a vinaigrette dressing.

TWOSOME TOSS
(See picture, p. 38)

Yield: 24 portions

Ingredients

BRUSSELS SPROUTS, FROZEN	2½ pounds
BOILING SALTED WATER	1 quart
OIL and VINEGAR DRESSING	1 quart
GREEN ONIONS, chopped	1 cup
PARSLEY, minced	1 cup
LETTUCE, ICEBERG, cut into cubes	5 1-pound heads
LETTUCE, ICEBERG, separated into leaves	1½ pounds

Procedure

1. Add unthawed sprouts to boiling salted water. Bring back to boil; cook until sprouts are crisp tender. (For 55 to 75 count per pound, allow about 5 minutes after water returns to boil. For 24 to 45 counts, allow about 10 minutes.)

2. Drain sprouts; cool. Cut lengthwise into halves.

3. Combine oil and vinegar dressing, onions and parsley. Pour over sprouts. Marinate, refrigerated, for several hours.

4. Toss sprout mixture with cubed lettuce. Serve in lettuce cups.

TROPICAL ONION-ORANGE SALAD

Yield: 48 portions

Ingredients

MIXED SALAD GREENS	3 gallons
FRESH ORANGE SLICES	1½ gallons
ONIONS, sliced	4 pounds
CELERY, diced	1 gallon
CHICKEN, julienne	5 pounds
SCALLIONS	4 bunches
VINAIGRETTE DRESSING	2 quarts

Procedure

1. Toss together salad greens, orange slices, onions and celery.

2. Just before serving, pile salad mixture into individual salad bowls. Top with chicken and scallions. Serve with dressing.

Note

If desired, sprinkle sieved hard cooked egg yolk over salad.

Avocado-Spinach Salad (Recipe, facing page)

General Foods Corp.

AVOCADO-SPINACH SALAD
(See picture, facing page)
Yield: approximately 12 portions

Ingredients

SPINACH, FRESH, torn or cut into bite-size pieces	2 quarts
LETTUCE, ICEBERG, coarsely cut	1½ quarts
AVOCADOS, peeled, diced	2
ONIONS, mild, sweet, thinly sliced	1 to 2
SALAD DRESSING, CHEESE GARLIC or GARLIC FRENCH	1 cup
BREAD CROUTONS, toasted	2 cups

Procedure

1. Combine spinach, lettuce, avocados and onions. Add salad dressing; toss lightly.
2. Add croutons; toss to mix.

ORANGE AND GREEN SALAD

Yield: 24 portions

Ingredients

CURLY ENDIVE	1 to 2 heads
SPINACH, fresh young	1 pound
VINEGAR, TARRAGON	½ cup
SUGAR	4 teaspoons
SALT	4 teaspoons
PAPRIKA	2 teaspoons
GARLIC CLOVES	3 to 4
SALAD OIL	1½ cups
ORANGE SECTIONS	1 quart
ONIONS, mild, sliced	3

Procedure

1. Tear endive and spinach into bite-size pieces. Chill.
2. Mix vinegar, sugar, salt and paprika. Add garlic cloves and salad oil. Let stand to blend flavors.
3. Just before serving, add orange sections and sliced onions to greens. Remove garlic from dressing; pour dressing over salad ingredients; toss lightly to mix.

GOLDEN NUGGET SALAD

Yield: approximately 24 portions

Ingredients

SALAD OIL	¾ cup
VINEGAR, WINE	½ cup
ONIONS, small, sliced and separated into rings	3
GARLIC CLOVES, peeled and strung on toothpick	3 to 4
SALT	1 tablespoon
PEPPER	¼ teaspoon
SUGAR	1 tablespoon
WHOLE KERNEL CORN, drained	3 No. 303 cans
RIPE OLIVES, sliced	1 cup
SALAD GREENS (lettuce, romaine, escarole, chicory) in bite-size pieces	1½ gallons

Procedure

1. Combine oil, vinegar, onions, garlic, seasonings, corn and ripe olives. Chill several hours to blend flavors. Remove garlic.

2. Add marinated corn to salad greens; toss lightly, adding salt and pepper as desired.

BACON 'N VEGETABLE SALAD

Yield: 24 2-cup portions

Ingredients

BACON, sliced	3 pounds
LETTUCE, torn in pieces	1 gallon
ROMAINE, torn in pieces	3 quarts
MIXED VEGETABLES, cooked, chilled	2¼ pounds
CELERY, sliced	1 quart
GREEN ONIONS, sliced	½ cup
EGGS, hard-cooked, sliced	12
OIL and VINEGAR DRESSING	3 cups

Procedure

1. Cook bacon until crisp; drain. Break into pieces.

2. Combine lettuce, romaine, mixed vegetables, celery and green onions. Toss with bacon and sliced eggs.

3. Serve with oil and vinegar dressing.

LETTUCE AND EGG SALAD

Yield: 16 5-ounce portions

Ingredients

LETTUCE HEARTS, cut in bite-size pieces	2 pounds
CELERY, cut in ¼-inch crescents	14 ounces
EGGS, hard-cooked, sliced	8 eggs
PEAS, cooked, drained	12 ounces
PIMIENTOES, chopped, drained	1 ounce
MAYONNAISE	14 ounces
SALT	1 teaspoon
PEPPER, WHITE	½ teaspoon
MUSTARD, DRY	½ teaspoon

Procedure

1. Combine lettuce, celery, eggs, peas and pimientoes.
2. Mix mayonnaise and seasonings.
3. Just before serving, add dressing to lettuce mixture; mix lightly but thoroughly.

GUACAMOLE SALAD

Yield: 6 to 8 portions

Ingredients

AVOCADOS, large, ripe	3
PEPPER, CAYENNE	1 teaspoon
VINEGAR, WHITE	2 tablespoons
ONION, minced	1 small
COOKING OIL	1 tablespoon
GARLIC, minced	2 cloves
GREEN PEPPERS, ORTEGA, finely chopped	1 7-ounce can
SALT	as needed

Procedure

1. Peel avocados, remove seeds; mash pulp lightly.
2. Blend cayenne with vinegar; blend in all other ingredients, adding salt to taste. Refrigerate until ready to serve.
3. Serve avocado mixture (guacamole) on top of bowls of tossed green salad (romaine, chicory and Belgian endive, tossed with French dressing). Garnish with tomato wedges (peeled); sprinkle with Parmesan cheese.

GREEN AND GOLD SALAD
(See picture, facing page)

Yield: 24 portions

Ingredients

LETTUCE, ICEBERG, torn into pieces	1¾ gallons
AVOCADOS, cut into rings	8 to 10
EGGS, hard-cooked, sliced	12 eggs
PECANS, chopped	2 cups
TART DRESSING*	as needed

Procedure

1. Place torn lettuce in individual salad bowls. Arrange avocado rings and egg slices on top. Sprinkle with pecans.
2. Serve with Tart Dressing or other favorite salad dressing.

*TART DRESSING

Yield: 1 quart

Ingredients

SALAD OIL	1 cup
LEMON JUICE	2 cups
SUGAR, CONFECTIONERS'	1 cup
VINEGAR	¾ cup
SALT	2 tablespoons
PAPRIKA	2 tablespoons
MUSTARD, DRY	1 tablespoon
ONION SALT	1½ teaspoons
PEPPER	1 teaspoon

Procedure

1. Blend ingredients until thoroughly mixed. Chill.

Green and Gold Salad (Recipe, facing page)

California Avocado Advisory Board

SPRING SALAD

Yield: 25 portions

Ingredients

FRESH SPINACH, coarsely cut	2-1/4 pounds
RADISHES, thinly sliced	3/4 pound (2-1/4 cups)
CUCUMBERS, chopped	3/4 pound (2-1/4 cups)
ONIONS, chopped	1 cup
FRENCH DRESSING	1 cup
GARLIC, minced	1/4 clove
SALT	1-1/2 teaspoons
VINEGAR	1/3 cup
EGGS, hard-cooked, chopped	5
PICKLES, SWEET, chopped	1 cup
PIMIENTOES, chopped	1/2 cup
GREEN PEPPERS, chopped	6 ounces (1-1/2 cups)

Procedure

1. Combine prepared vegetables. Cover and chill.

2. Mix French dressing, garlic, salt, vinegar, eggs, pickles, pimientoes and green peppers.

3. Just before serving, toss French dressing mixture and vegetables together lightly.

CHEF'S TOSSED SALAD

Yield: 50 portions

Ingredients

RADISHES, sliced 1/8-inch thick	2 cups
CARROTS, shredded	1 quart
RED CABBAGE, cut 1-inch long, 1/8-inch wide	2 cups
GREEN PEPPERS, cut 1-inch x 1/4-inch	2 peppers
LETTUCE, ICEBERG, 1-inch squares	3 quarts
ESCAROLE, 1-inch pieces	3 quarts
ROMAINE, 1-inch pieces	3 quarts
ENDIVE (chicory), 1-inch pieces	2 quarts

Procedure

1. Toss ingredients together in large bowl. Refrigerate. Do not mix more than enough for one meal. To mix smaller amounts, combine radishes, carrots, red cabbage and green peppers. Mix greens. Combine, as needed, using one part radish mixture to 5½ parts greens.

For individual salads: Fill bowl with salad mixture; garnish with a wedge of tomato or a slice of beet, cut julienne. Serve with 1 ounce of dressing.

Note

If any one of the leaf greens are not used, increase the three kinds used to make up the required amount (11 quarts).

EAST INDIAN SALAD SPECIAL

Yield: 50 portions

Ingredients

CURLY ENDIVE, torn into bite-size pieces	4 bunches
ORANGES, large, peeled and sectioned	24
ONIONS, BERMUDA or RED, sliced and separated into rings	4
OLIVES, GREEN, PIMIENTO-STUFFED, sliced	2 cups
COCONUT, flaked	1 to 2 cups
SALAD OIL	3 cups
VINEGAR	1 cup
SUGAR	2½ tablespoons
SALT	1½ tablespoons
PAPRIKA	1 tablespoon
CURRY POWDER	2 teaspoons
INSTANT GRANULATED GARLIC	1 teaspoon

Procedure

1. Combine endive, orange sections, onion rings, olive slices and coconut; toss lightly.

2. Combine remaining ingredients; mix well. Pour over salad mixture; toss again to coat greens and fruits.

Dark Greens Make Effective Garnish

Western Growers Association

MARINATED ITALIAN SALAD

MARINADE
Yield: for 36 bowls

Ingredients

CELERY, diced	16 pounds
OLIVES, SALAD, drained	1 gallon
GIARDINERA, undrained	1 gallon
PEPPERONCINI, undrained	1 gallon
CAPERS, undrained	2 quarts
GARLIC, tied in bag, crushed	10 cloves
VINEGAR, RED WINE	1 gallon
OLIVE OIL	1 gallon
SALAD OIL	1 gallon
OREGANO LEAVES	2 ounces

Procedure

1. Combine ingredients in a 15-gallon stainless steel container or crock; marinate at least 24 hours.

SALAD BOWL
Yield: 30 portions

Ingredients

LETTUCE, cut in bite-size pieces	5 heads
TOMATOES, cut in half crosswise, then in wedges	2 pounds
MARINADE	1 quart
ANCHOVIES	4 ounces
OLIVES, BLACK	1 cup
MARINADE	1 cup

Procedure

1. Place lettuce and tomatoes in bowl. Pour over first amount of marinade; toss so that oil shines on lettuce.

2. Cut anchovies in half; arrange on top of bowl. Scatter ripe olives on top of bowl. Sprinkle with remaining 1 cup marinade.

Salad Arranged on Heart of Romaine

Western Growers Assn.

Arranged Green Salads

THE TOSSED green salads lend themselves to tableside prepar-ation with impressive flourishes of the peppermill and other fanfare. Arranged green salads, on the other hand, are com-pleted prior to service and at their perkiest best are ready for presentation on super-cool plates. The most successful salads of this type give an impression of casualness. They never look belabored or the least bit contrived.

The various kinds of lettuce, along with Belgian endive and watercress, are foremost candidates for these salads. Ice-berg is particularly versatile. You can present it as a wedge, a slice or shredded. You can combine it with cress. Cradle a portion of shredded lettuce in a deep lettuce cup; tuck a nose-gay of cress in at one side. Make a similar arrangement with an iceberg wedge.

The inner leaves of Boston lettuce also make a pleasing salad when arranged as a nest with watercress beside it, and given the colorful accent of a tomato wedge. Or, when com-bined with a simple oil and vinegar dressing, and garnished with sieved yolk of egg.

Whole heads of Bibb lettuce, when small, make elegant salads. Larger heads are attractive cut in half. A scattering of toasted sliced almonds adds a chic garnish that tastes good too. Small heads of romaine also make smart salads, presented as a half- or quarter-head with a comely bit of garnish to set them off.

A Belgian endive salad adds a note of luxury to the finest meal. The leaves (separated from the head) need only a light coating of dressing and a suspicion of herbs. Endive and marinated tomato slices produce another classic; endive and watercress a similar delight.

HEARTY MARINATED MUSHROOM SALAD PLATE

Yield: 48 portions

Ingredients

MUSHROOMS, FRESH, sliced*	6 quarts
CELERY, diced	1 gallon
OIL, salad	1 quart
VINEGAR, wine	2 cups
ONION FLAKES	½ cup
SALT	3 tablespoons
OREGANO LEAVES	4 teaspoons
INSTANT MINCED GARLIC	2 teaspoons
SUGAR	2 teaspoons
PEPPER, BLACK	2 teaspoons
ROMAINE LETTUCE	4 heads
HAM, julienne	2 pounds
TURKEY, julienne	2 pounds
CHEESE, SWISS, julienne	2 pounds
TOMATO WEDGES	6 pounds
RADISH ROSES	2 pounds
PARSLEY (optional)	as needed

Procedure

1. Place mushrooms and celery in large bowl.

2. Combine oil, vinegar and seasonings; mix well. Pour over mushroom mixture; toss gently. Cover; refrigerate 6 to 8 hours or overnight.

3. Arrange romaine leaves on salad plate. Spoon marinated mushrooms in center. Arrange ham, turkey, cheese, tomato wedges and radish roses around mushrooms. Garnish with parsley, if desired.

*Or, canned mushrooms, drained, 1 No. 10 can.

Strawberry Cottage Delight (Recipe, below)
Twosome Toss (Recipe, p. 23)
Hearts of Lettuce Espanol (Recipe, facing page)

Western Iceberg Lettuce, Inc.

STRAWBERRY COTTAGE DELIGHT
(See picture, above)

Yield: 24 portions

Ingredients

LETTUCE, ICEBERG (1-pound heads)	4 to 5
COTTAGE CHEESE, CREAMED	3 pounds
SOUR CREAM	2 pounds
STRAWBERRIES, sliced, sweetened, fresh or frozen, thawed	1½ pounds

Procedure

1. Slice lettuce across heads into 24 "rafts."
2. Combine cottage cheese and sour cream; fold in strawberries.
3. Ladle approximately 3 ounces cheese mixture over each "raft" of lettuce. Garnish with a whole fresh strawberry, if desired.

HEARTS OF LETTUCE ESPANOL
(See picture, facing page)

Yield: 24 portions, 1½ quarts dressing

Ingredients

OLIVES, GREEN, PIMIENTO-STUFFED	1 cup (5½ ounces)
EGGS, hard-cooked	4
MAYONNAISE	1 quart
CREAM, heavy	1 cup
CATSUP	½ cup
CHIVES, minced	¼ cup
LETTUCE, ICEBERG	24 wedges
OLIVES, GREEN, PIMIENTO-STUFFED (for garnish)	48

Procedure

1. Coarsely chop first amount of olives.
2. Chop eggs fine.
3. Combine olives, eggs, mayonnaise, cream, catsup and chives.
4. Ladle 2 ounces dressing over each lettuce wedge. Garnish with whole olives.

FRENCH MIMOSA SALAD

Yield: 24 portions

Ingredients

LETTUCE, BOSTON	4 heads
EGGS, hard-cooked, shelled	16
PARSLEY, chopped	¾ cup

Procedure

1. Separate lettuce leaves; wash; chill.
2. Halve eggs; separate whites from yolks.
3. Arrange 2 or 3 lettuce leaves on individual plates; sprinkle with parsley.
4. Press egg whites and then yolks through a sieve over the salad.
5. Serve with French dressing.

CHIFFONADE SALAD GARNI

Yield: 50 portions

Ingredients

FRESH COOKED BEETS	4 pounds
CELERY	1½ bunches
ONIONS	1½ pounds
WATERCRESS	1 bunch
ROMAINE	3 heads
ESCAROLE	1 pound
CHICORY	1 head
ENDIVE	1 pound
HERBED DRESSING	1½ to 2 cups
HARD-COOKED EGGS, chopped	4

Procedure

1. Cut beets and celery in julienne and onions in rings and marinate separately in a French dressing for 1½ hours.

2. Cut greens in bite-size pieces. Toss together with dressing.

3. Serve on cold plates. Garnish with the marinated celery, beets and onion rings.

4. Sprinkle chopped egg over top.

CHIFFONADE SALAD

Yield: 24 portions

Ingredients

LETTUCE, wedges or slices	24
ONIONS, thinly sliced	2 medium
EGGS, hard-cooked, chopped	4
PIMIENTOES, diced	1 cup
CHEESE, CHEDDAR, shredded	3 cups
FRENCH DRESSING	2 cups

Procedure

1. Arrange lettuce on chilled salad plates.

2. Combine remaining ingredients; serve over lettuce.

Salads with Hot Dressing

A SELECT group of green salads departs from the usual to combine with a dressing that goes on hot. Of these, the Madras Bowl and Imperial Pork Salad are eminently suited to tableside making, offering opportunities for clever showmanship from beginning to end.

To anyone who hasn't watched the procedure before, the unexpected addition of a hot dressing to cold, crisp greens initiates a curious wonder. But the heat of the dressing doesn't entirely destroy the crispness. Served at once (as it must be), a little warm and still holding a definite crunch, this form of tossed salad is an intriguing experience.

Madras Bowl (Recipe, facing page)

MADRAS BOWL
(See picture, facing page)

Yield: 4 portions

Ingredients

ICEBERG LETTUCE (heart portion) cut in cubes, SPINACH LEAVES AND MIXED GREENS* to make	1½ quarts
TOMATO, cut in wedges	1
Or CHERRY TOMATOES, halved	8 to 12
Or AVOCADO, sliced	1
VINEGAR, CIDER	3 tablespoons
OLIVE OIL	1/3 cup
ONIONS, finely chopped	2 tablespoons
SALT	1/2 teaspoon
CURRY POWDER	1/2 to 3/4 teaspoon
SUGAR	pinch
RIPE OLIVES, pitted whole	12 to 16
BACON, crumbled	as needed
EGG YOLKS, hard-cooked, sieved	as needed

Procedure

1. Place greens and tomato in salad bowl.
2. Combine vinegar, oil, onion and seasonings in blazer pan of chafing dish or small saucepan; bring to a boil. Add olives; heat through.
3. Pour hot dressing over greens; toss well. Garnish portions with bacon and egg yolks.

*Use any preferred combination of sturdy type salad greens (romaine, chicory, escarole, etc.) with the lettuce hearts and spinach.

Variation

For Caliente Bowl, substitute wine vinegar for cider vinegar, chili powder for curry and crumbled corn chips for bacon.

IMPERIAL PORK SALAD

Yield: 4 portions

Ingredients

LETTUCE, WESTERN ICEBERG, shredded	1 head
PARSLEY, chopped	1/2 cup
PORK, cooked, sliced	6 ounces
SALAD OIL	2/3 cup
RED WINE VINEGAR	2/3 cup
SOY SAUCE	2 tablespoons
MUSTARD, DRY	2 teaspoons
SEASONED SALT	1 teaspoon
PEPPER, WHITE, ground	few dashes
SESAME SEEDS, lightly toasted	as needed

Procedure

1. Combine lettuce and parsley in salad bowl.

2. Cut pork into thin strips about 1-inch long.

3. To prepare sauce in kitchen or at tableside, combine oil, vinegar, soy sauce, mustard, seasoned salt and pepper in blazer of chafing dish.

4. Bring to a boil; cook about 1 minute. Add pork; heat through.

5. To serve, turn the very hot sauce into the salad bowl; toss quickly.

6. Serve at once; sprinkle each portion with sesame seed.

Note

Serve with hot crusty bread as a luncheon salad. Or, as a course for a Chinese-style dinner.

CHOPPED SPINACH WITH BACON DRESSING

Yield: 25 portions

Ingredients

BACON, cut in ½-inch pieces	10 ounces
FLOUR	1/3 cup
SUGAR	1/3 cup
SALT	1 tablespoon
BACON FAT	1/3 cup
MILK, hot	3 cups
EGGS, beaten	1 cup (5)
VINEGAR	1/2 cup
SPINACH, raw, coarsely chopped	2 pounds

Procedure

1. Fry bacon until crisp. Drain. Reserve fat needed for dressing.

2. Add flour, sugar and salt to bacon fat. Blend in milk. Cook over low heat until thickened, stirring constantly.

3. Add the hot mixture slowly to beaten eggs, beating slowly. Add vinegar and bacon.

4. Pour hot dressing over spinach; toss to mix.

Sparkling Gelatin Molds

General Foods Corp.

GELATIN SALADS

COLORFUL, cool-looking and refreshing, molded salads can carry off the honors as the most inviting section of the meal.

Fashioned with vegetables, fruit or heartier ingredients (such as meat, cheese, fish and eggs), molded salads can be served in a variety of ways. Many are suited for presenting as appetizers. Countless others are ideal as "side salads" to accompany and enliven the main course. Still others rate as full-fledged entrees in themselves. They bid for listing with the luncheon items, for promoting with the cold buffet.

Commonplace ingredients become more exciting when molded. Yet success with either plain or flavored gelatin is easy to achieve.

A few pointers to improve the know-how:

DISSOLVE GELATIN thoroughly.

CUT VEGETABLES, FRUITS, AND SUCH neatly and attractively. Remember that very large pieces may complicate unmolding and serving.

KEEP THE MEASURE of the added ingredients less than, or equal to, the measure of the liquid gelatin.

CHILL GELATIN until thick and syrupy. (A spoon drawn through should leave a definite trace.) To hasten chill-

ing, follow directions for Quick Preparation of Gelatin below.

FOLD INGREDIENTS into gelatin, just enough to distribute evenly. (Overmixing may soften gelatin. In addition, it can cause air bubbles which impair the clear, sparkly look.)

TURN INTO MOLDS (Fancy molds are really not needed though they do give a prettier effect). In lieu of them, pour gelatin into pans to cut into squares.

CHILL UNTIL FIRM (Gelatin should not bulge or move when you tip the mold.)

DIP MOLDS QUICKLY, just to the top, in warm water. SHAKE THE MOLD slightly to free the salad. PLACE on a chilled plate with fresh perky greens.

Your salad is ready to go!

QUICK PREPARATION OF GELATIN
(For Salads and Desserts)

Yield: 5 to 6 quarts (with fruit)

Ingredients

GELATIN, ANY FLAVOR	1½ pounds (3½ cups)
WATER, boiling	1½ quarts
ICE, chipped or finely crushed	2½ quarts
COLD WATER OR FRUIT JUICE	as needed

Procedure

1. Dissolve gelatin in boiling water.

2. Measure ice; add enough cold water or fruit juice to just cover the ice in the measure. Add ice and liquid to gelatin; stir until ice is melted. (Gelatin will begin to thicken almost at once. Speed of thickening depends upon the proportion of ice to water and size of ice particles.)

3. As soon as gelatin is slightly thickened, fold in drained cut fruit (except fresh pineapple). Allow 2 quarts of fruit for each gallon of gelatin.

To use this method in other gelatin recipes:

1. Measure 1/3 of the liquid called for in the recipe (or measure up to 1/2 of the liquid, if that makes a more practical measurement).

2. Bring to a boil; add to gelatin; stir until dissolved.

3. Measure rest of required liquid as crushed ice; add cold water just to cover the ice in the measuring container.

4. Add to gelatin; stir until ice is melted and gelatin thickened. Proceed as directed for rest of recipe.

SALMON SALAD APPETIZER
WITH ROQUEFORT DRESSING

Yield: 42 3-ounce portions

Ingredients

GELATINE, UNFLAVORED	2 ounces
WATER, cold	1 cup
MILK, hot	1-1/2 quarts
SALMON, flaked	2 pounds
CELERY, finely cut	4-1/2 cups
GREEN PEPPERS, chopped	1/2 cup
ONION, minced	1/4 cup
PIMIENTOES, diced	1/3 cup
SWEET PICKLE RELISH	1 cup
LEMON JUICE	½ cup
SALT	2 teaspoons
MAYONNAISE	2 cups

Procedure

1. Soak gelatine in cold water 5 minutes. Add hot milk gradually, stirring until gelatine is dissolved. (If milk starts to curdle, place over cold water and beat with rotary beater until smooth.) Cool.

2. Combine remaining ingredients. Mix with cooled gelatine mixture. Chill until slightly thickened, stirring occasionally.

3. Turn into loaf pans. Chill until firm.

4. Unmold. Cut into thick slices, then cut slices in half. Serve on crisp lettuce with Roquefort dressing.* Garnish with cress, if desired.

*ROQUEFORT DRESSING

Yield: approximately 1¼ quarts

Ingredients

MAYONNAISE	3 cups
LEMON JUICE	¾ cup
CELERY SEED	1 tablespoon
RQOUEFORT CHEESE, crumbled	3 cups

Procedure

1. Combine mayonnaise, lemon juice and celery seed.

2. Add Roquefort; mix well.

ASPARAGUS AND EGG SOUFFLE SALAD

Yield: 32 4-ounce portions

Ingredients

GELATIN, LEMON	12 ounces
WATER, hot	1½ quarts
VINEGAR	½ cup
MAYONNAISE	2 cups
SALT	2 teaspoons
PEPPER	¼ teaspoon
EGGS, hard-cooked, diced	1 quart
ASPARAGUS, cooked (1-inch pieces)	1 quart
ONIONS, finely chopped	¼ cup

Procedure

1. Dissolve gelatin in hot water. Blend in vinegar, mayonnaise, salt and pepper.

2. Chill until slightly thickened (over crushed ice or in refrigerator). Beat until fluffy.

3. Fold in eggs, asparagus and onions. If necessary, chill a few minutes to thicken mixture enough to hold eggs and asparagus in even distribution.

4. Pour into individual molds or shallow pans. Chill until firm.

5. Unmold or cut into squares. Serve on crisp salad greens.

TUNA-OLIVE MOUSSE ➝

Yield: 50 portions

Ingredients

WATER	1½ cups
LEMON JUICE	¾ cup
GELATINE, UNFLAVORED	3 ounces
TUNA, drained and flaked	6 pounds
VINEGAR, TARRAGON	1 cup
SOUR CREAM	1½ quarts
MAYONNAISE	3 cups
OLIVES, PIMIENTO-STUFFED, chopped	3 cups

MOLDED CHICKEN A LA KING SALAD

Yield: 26 ½-cup portions

Ingredients

GELATINE, UNFLAVORED	6 tablespoons
WATER, cold	1-1/2 cups
CREAM OF CHICKEN SOUP, CONDENSED	1 50-ounce can
MAYONNAISE	1 cup
LEMON JUICE	1/3 cup
SALT	1/2 teaspoon
CHICKEN, cooked, diced	1 quart
CELERY, chopped	1-1/2 cups
PIMIENTOES, chopped	1/2 cup
GREEN PEPPERS, chopped	1/2 cup
ONION, grated	3 to 4 tablespoons

Procedure

1. Soften gelatine in cold water. Melt over low heat, stirring constantly.

2. Blend soup with mayonnaise, lemon juice and salt. Stir in gelatine.

3. Chill until slightly thickened. Fold in remaining ingredients.

4. Chill in individual 4-ounce molds until firm.

5. Unmold; serve on crisp salad greens.

Procedure

1. Combine water and lemon juice; soften gelatine in the liquid. Heat over hot water until gelatine is dissolved.

2. Combine tuna, vinegar, sour cream, mayonnaise and olives. Add gelatine; mix thoroughly.

3. Turn into individual molds, buffet molds or 12-inch by 20-inch pan. Chill until firm.

4. Unmold or cut squares. Serve on crisp salad greens. Garnish with additional olives, lemon and tomato wedges, if desired.

JELLIED CURRIED EGG SALAD

Yield: 1 gallon, 32 ½-cup portions

Ingredients

GELATINE, UNFLAVORED	2 ounces
WATER, cold	2 cups
WATER, hot	3 cups
MAYONNAISE	2-1/2 cups
EGGS, hard-cooked, coarsely cut	30
GREEN PEPPERS, chopped	1 cup
CELERY, finely cut	3 cups
PIMIENTOES, chopped	1 cup
PICKLE RELISH	3/4 cup
SALT	2 tablespoons
CURRY POWDER	2 tablespoons
LEMON JUICE	2/3 cup

Procedure

1. Soak gelatine in cold water 5 minutes. Add hot water; stir until gelatine is dissolved. Gradually add to mayonnaise, stirring to blend. (If mixture starts to curdle, beat with rotary beater until smooth.) Chill until slightly thickened.

2. Fold in remaining ingredients. Turn into loaf pan or individual molds. Chill until firm.

3. Unmold; cut loaf mold in slices. Serve on crisp salad greens.

Note

Individual ring molds may be filled with shrimp, lobster, chicken, or mixed vegetable salad.

JELLIED HAM AND PINEAPPLE SALAD

Yield: 48 portions

Ingredients

GELATINE, UNFLAVORED	4 ounces
CHICKEN BROTH	2 quarts
PINEAPPLE, CRUSHED	1 No. 10 can
LEMON JUICE	1 cup
PREPARED HORSERADISH	4 ounces
SALT	1 teaspoon
LIQUID RED PEPPER SEASONING	1/4 teaspoon
DILL WEED	1/2 teaspoon
GREEN ONIONS, finely chopped	4 ounces
PIMIENTOES, finely chopped	8 ounces
HAM, cooked, diced	1 pound, 5 ounces
PREPARED MUSTARD	4 teaspoons
MAYONNAISE	1 quart
CREAM, HEAVY (for whipping)	1 quart

Procedure

1. Soften gelatine in chicken broth. Place over low heat; stir until dissolved.

2. Add pineapple, lemon juice, seasonings, onion, pimiento and ham. Chill until slightly thickened.

3. Combine mustard with mayonnaise.

4. Whip cream.

5. Add mayonnaise mixture to slightly thickened gelatine. Fold in whipped cream.

6. Turn into individual molds or 2 pans, 12-inch by 20-inch by 2-inch. Chill until firm.

7. Unmold or cut into squares. Serve on crisp greens.

OLIVE RELISH ASPIC

Yield: 24 portions

Ingredients

GELATIN, LEMON	1¾ cups (12 ounces)
WATER, hot	1¾ quarts
SALT	2½ teaspoons
VINEGAR	¾ cup
RIPE OLIVES, pitted, coarsely chopped	1 No. 1 tall can
CABBAGE, shredded	3 cups (10 ounces)
CARROTS, shredded	1½ cups (5 ounces)
CELERY, thinly sliced	1½ cups (5 ounces)
GREEN PEPPER, thinly sliced	1
PIMIENTO, medium, diced	1

Procedure

1. Dissolve gelatin in hot water; add salt and vinegar. Chill until slightly thickened.

2. Fold in coarsely chopped olives, cabbage, carrot, celery, green pepper and pimiento. Turn into individual molds or in shallow pan; chill until firm.

3. Unmold or cut into squares. Serve on crisp salad greens.

TOMATO ASPIC

Yield: 32 4-ounce portions

Ingredients

TOMATO JUICE	3 quarts
SUGAR, GRANULATED	¼ cup
SALT	1 tablespoon
ONION, chopped	½ cup
CELERY TOPS	2 cups
BAY LEAVES	2
WHOLE CLOVES	½ teaspoon
PEPPERCORNS	¼ teaspoon
GELATINE, UNFLAVORED	½ cup
TOMATO JUICE	1 quart
LEMON JUICE	¾ cup

Procedure

1. Combine first amount of tomato juice with sugar, salt, onion, celery tops, bay leaves, cloves, and peppercorns in a heavy saucepan. Cover; simmer 15 minutes.

2. Soak gelatine in remaining tomato juice 5 minutes.

3. Strain hot tomato mixture. Add to gelatine; stir until dissolved. Add lemon juice.

4. Turn into individual molds or shallow 10-inch by 12-inch pans. Chill until firm.

5. Unmold or cut in squares. Serve on crisp greens with mayonnaise or cottage cheese.

CHICKEN ROYAL SALAD

Yield: 40 ½-cup portions

Ingredients

GELATINE, UNFLAVORED	5 tablespoons
WATER, cold	2 cups
CREAM OF CHICKEN SOUP, CONDENSED	2 cups
SCALLIONS, with tops, minced	½ cup
CHICKEN, diced	1 quart
SALT	1 teaspoon
SALT	1 tablespoon
PASCAL CELERY, chopped	2 cups
MAYONNAISE	1 cup
COTTAGE CHEESE, CREAMED	6 pounds
PEPPER	¼ teaspoon

Procedure

1. Soften gelatine in cold water. Dissolve over low heat, stirring constantly.

2. Heat soup until bubbling. Remove from heat; add scallions, chicken and first amount of salt.

3. Gradually stir in dissolved gelatine. Cool to room temperature.

4. Sprinkle remaining salt over celery. Add mayonnaise, mix well. Add cottage cheese and pepper; mix well.

5. Combine cooled gelatine mixture with cheese mixture. Pour into individual molds or shallow pans. Chill until firm.

6. Serve on crisp lettuce. Garnish with ripe olives and carrot curls.

MILLIE'S CRAB SALAD

Yield: 36 portions

Ingredients

GELATIN, LEMON	1 pound
WATER, boiling	1 quart
SALT	2 teaspoons
ONION, grated	2 tablespoons
LEMON JUICE	¼ cup
MAYONNAISE	2 cups
EGGS, hard-cooked, chopped	8
CHEESE, CHEDDAR, grated	1 pound
GREEN PEPPERS, finely minced	2 tablespoons
CELERY, finely chopped	1 cup
PECANS, finely chopped	1 cup
CRABMEAT	2 pounds
CREAM, WHIPPING	2 cups

Procedure

1. Dissolve gelatin in boiling water. Add salt, onion and lemon juice. Chill until slightly thickened.

2. Add mayonnaise; blend well.

3. Fold in eggs, cheese, green pepper, celery, pecans and crabmeat.

4. Whip cream until thick and shiny. Fold into gelatin mixture.

5. Turn into individual molds; chill until firm.

6. Unmold; serve on crisp salad greens. Garnish salads with mayonnaise and a lemon wedge.

DEVILED EGG SALAD

Yield: 52 ½-cup portions

Ingredients

GELATIN, LEMON	1½ pounds (3½ cups)
SALT	2 tablespoons
CELERY SALT	2 teaspoons
PAPRIKA	2 teaspoons
WATER, boiling	2 quarts
WATER, cold	1¾ quarts
VINEGAR	¾ cup
MUSTARD, PREPARED	6 tablespoons
MAYONNAISE	3 cups
EGGS, hard-cooked, finely chopped	24 (2 quarts)

Procedure

1. Mix gelatin, salt, celery salt and paprika. Dissolve in boiling water. Add cold water and vinegar. Chill until slightly thickened.

2. Blend mustard into mayonnaise. Whip into slightly thickened gelatin. Fold in chopped eggs.

3. Pour into individual molds or shallow pans. Chill until firm.

4. Unmold or cut into squares. Serve on crisp salad greens. Garnish with pimiento strips or parsley sprigs.

JELLIED COLE SLAW ⟶

Yield: 42 3-ounce portions

Ingredients

GELATIN, LEMON	12 ounces (1¾ cups)
WATER, hot	1½ quarts
VINEGAR	½ cup
MAYONNAISE	2 cups
SALT	1 teaspoon
PEPPER	¼ teaspoon
ONIONS, finely chopped	¼ cup
CABBAGE, finely chopped	2 quarts
GREEN PEPPERS, finely chopped	½ cup
CELERY SEED	1 teaspoon

SPINACH COTTAGE CHEESE SOUFFLE SALAD

Yield: 60 ½-cup portions

Ingredients

GELATIN, LEMON	1½ pounds (3½ cups)
WATER, hot (140° to 160°F.)	3 quarts
VINEGAR	¾ cup
MAYONNAISE	3 cups
SALT	1 tablespoon
PEPPER	½ teaspoon
SPINACH, RAW, chopped	2 quarts (¾ pound)
COTTAGE CHEESE	4 pounds
CELERY, diced	3 cups (14 ounces)
ONIONS, finely chopped	½ cup (3 ounces)

Procedure

1. Dissolve gelatin in hot water. Add vinegar, mayonnaise, salt and pepper. Blend with beater. Chill until slightly thickened.

2. Beat mixture until fluffy.

3. Combine remaining ingredients; fold into gelatin mixture.

4. Pour into individual molds or shallow pans. Chill until firm.

5. Unmold or cut into squares. Serve on crisp salad greens. Garnish with radish roses or tomato wedges, if desired.

Procedure

1. Dissolve gelatin in hot water. Add vinegar, mayonnaise, salt and pepper; blend with beater.

2. Chill mixture until slightly thickened; beat on mixer until fluffy.

3. Combine remaining ingredients; fold into gelatin. Chill until mixture is thick enough to hold vegetables in even distribution. Turn into pans or small individual molds. Chill until firm. Cut into squares or unmold. Serve on leaves of lettuce, chicory or cress.

MOLDED SPRING SALAD

Yield: 32 ½-cup portions

Ingredients

GELATIN, LIME	1 pound
WATER, boiling	2-1/4 quarts
VINEGAR	1/2 cup
SALT	1 tablespoon
CUCUMBERS, finely diced	1-1/4 quarts
CELERY, finely cut	1 quart
SCALLIONS, finely cut	2 cups

Procedure

1. Dissolve gelatin in hot water. Add vinegar and salt. Chill until slightly thickened.
2. Combine vegetables; fold into slightly thickened gelatin.
3. Turn into individual molds or shallow pans. Chill until firm.
4. Unmold or cut into squares. Serve on crisp greens. Garnish with sour cream mayonnaise.

MOLDED GAZPACHO SALAD

Yield: 20 ½-cup portions

Ingredients

GELATINE, UNFLAVORED	6 tablespoons
WATER, cold	2-1/2 cups
TOMATO SOUP, CONDENSED	1 51-ounce can
VINEGAR, CIDER	1/4 cup
SALT	1/4 teaspoon
HOT PEPPER SAUCE	12 drops
CUCUMBERS, chopped	1-1/2 cups
GREEN PEPPERS, finely chopped	1-1/2 cups
ONIONS, finely minced	1/3 to 1/2 cup

Procedure

1. Soften gelatine in cold water. Melt over low heat, stirring constantly.
2. Blend in soup, vinegar, salt and hot pepper sauce. Chill until slightly thickened.
3. Fold in remaining ingredients. Chill in individual molds until firm.
4. Unmold. Serve on crisp salad greens.

TART COTTAGE CHEESE ASPIC

Yield: 50 ½-cup portions

Ingredients

COCKTAIL VEGETABLE JUICE	3 46-ounce cans
GELATINE, UNFLAVORED	3/4 cup
VINEGAR, TARRAGON	3/4 to 1 cup
ONION, grated	3 tablespoons
COTTAGE CHEESE	3 pounds
CUCUMBERS, ¼-inch cubes	3 cups

Procedure

1. Measure out 2 cups of vegetable juice into a saucepan; sprinkle gelatine over top. Place over low heat; stir until gelatine is completely dissolved.

2. Add remaining juice, vinegar and onion; chill until slightly thickened.

3. Fold in cheese and cucumber. Pour into individual molds or two 12-inch by 20-inch by 2½-inch pans. Chill until firm.

SUNSET SALAD

Yield: 24 portions

Ingredients

GELATIN, LEMON	2 cups
WATER, boiling	1 quart
PINEAPPLE SYRUP AND COLD WATER	1 quart
LEMON JUICE	1/2 cup
SALT	1 tablespoon
CARROTS, raw, grated	1 quart
CELERY, finely sliced	2 cups
PINEAPPLE, crushed, drained	1-1/4 quarts

Procedure

1. Dissolve gelatin in hot water.

2. Add the cold liquid (syrup drained from the pineapple and water). Chill until slightly thickened.

3. Add remaining ingredients; pour into individual molds or a 10-inch by 12-inch pan. Chill until firm.

4. Serve on shredded lettuce with mayonnaise mixed with sour cream.

CARDINAL SALAD

Yield: 44 ½-cup portions

Ingredients

GELATIN, LEMON	1½ pounds
SALT	1½ teaspoons
WATER, boiling	2 quarts
BEET JUICE	1½ quarts
VINEGAR	1 cup
LEMON JUICE	6 tablespoons
HORSERADISH, grated	2 tablespoons
CELERY, finely chopped	1 quart
BEETS, cooked, finely chopped	1½ quarts

Procedure

1. Dissolve gelatin and salt in boiling water.
2. Add beet juice, vinegar, lemon juice and horseradish. Chill until slightly thickened.
3. Fold in celery and beets.
4. Pour into individual molds or shallow pans; chill until firm.
5. Unmold or cut into squares. Serve on watercress or other salad greens.

BUFFET SHRIMP CHEESE MOLD ➝

Yield: 24 portions

Ingredients

GELATINE, UNFLAVORED	¼ cup
CONSOMME MADRILENE, CANNED	2½ quarts
SHRIMP, JUMBO, drained	6 4½- to 5-ounce cans
HORSERADISH, PREPARED	3 tablespoons
MAYONNAISE	1 cup
CELERY, thinly sliced	1½ cups
GREEN ONIONS, thinly sliced	½ cup
GREEN PEPPER, diced	½ cup
CUCUMBERS, diced	1 cup
COTTAGE CHEESE	1½ quarts

PERFECTION SALAD

Yield: 32 portions

Ingredients

GELATINE, UNFLAVORED	2 ounces
WATER, cold	1 quart
SUGAR	2 cups
SALT	4 teaspoons
WATER, cold	1½ quarts
VINEGAR	2 cups
LEMON JUICE	½ cup
CABBAGE, finely shredded	1½ quarts
CELERY, chopped	1¼ quarts
GREEN PEPPERS, chopped	1 cup
PIMIENTOES, cut in small pieces	½ cup

Procedure

1. Sprinkle gelatine over first amount of water in a deep saucepan. Place over medium heat; stir until gelatine dissolves.

2. Remove from heat; add sugar and salt; stir until dissolved.

3. Add remaining cold water, vinegar and lemon juice. Chill until slightly thickened.

4. Add remaining ingredients. Turn into molds or a 12-inch by 20-inch by 2-inch pan. Chill until firm.

5. Unmold or cut into squares. Serve on crisp salad greens.

Procedure

1. Soften gelatine in 2 cups of the consomme. Heat remaining consomme to boiling; add softened gelatine, stirring to dissolve. Cool.

2. Arrange drained shrimp in a single layer in bottoms of two 2-quart shallow molds.

3. Pour gelatine mixture over shrimp to cover, allowing about 2 cups for each mold. Chill until almost firm.

4. Combine remaining ingredients with remaining gelatine mixture; chill until partially thickened.

5. Spoon mixture over shrimp layer in molds. Chill until firm.

6. Unmold. Garnish with crisp salad greens.

Frozen Gelatin with Fruit

National Cherry Growers & Industries Foundation

Fruit Gelatin Salads

ALMOST any fruit, fresh, frozen or canned, is good in a gelatin salad. (But use only cooked or canned pineapple.) Two quarts of cut fruit to a gallon of gelatin makes a pleasing ratio.

For most recipes, chill gelatin to an unbeaten egg consistency before adding the fruit. Carefully fold the well drained fruit into the gelatin, distributing it evenly without creating air bubbles.

Self-layering fruit salads are an exception to the rule. They require adding the fruit while the gelatin is still in the liquid stage. This scheme takes advantage of the fact that some fruits sink while others float. Simply turn the dissolved gelatin into the pan. Add one fruit that is heavy enough to sink, and another that is light enough to float. Give it a stir to mix evenly; chill until firm; portion. That's all there is to it! The fruits separate before the gelatin sets and come out in two layers with a clear strip of gelatin between.

FRUITS THAT SINK: cooked prunes; canned fruits such as plums, pineapple, pears, apricots, raspberries, peaches, mandarin oranges, Royal Anne and dark sweet cherries.

FRUITS THAT FLOAT: fresh pitted Bing cherries; diced apples; grapefruit and orange sections; cantaloupe and honey-

dew cubes; fresh raspberries; fresh strawberry halves; fresh peach, pear and banana slices; broken nut meats; marshmallows; halved and seeded grapes.

GINGER PEAR SALAD

Yield: 48 ½-cup portions

Ingredients

GELATINE, UNFLAVORED	2½ ounces
SUGAR	2 cups
SALT	1 teaspoon
SWEET CIDER, cold*	1¼ quarts
LEMON JUICE	¼ cup
GINGERALE	2 quarts
PEARS (heavy syrup)	2 No. 10 cans
GINGER, CANDIED, finely diced	4 ounces

Procedure

1. Mix gelatine, sugar and salt in a saucepan. Add cold cider; heat and stir until dissolved.

2. Add lemon juice and 1 quart of gingerale. Chill to consistency of unbeaten egg whites.

3. Drain pears thoroughly; cut in ½-inch cubes; let drain until ready to use.

4. Add remaining 1 quart of gingerale to slightly thickened gelatine mixture. Fold in drained diced pears and candied ginger.

5. Pour into individual molds or shallow pans. Chill until firm. Unmold or cut into squares. Serve on crisp salad greens with mayonnaise or sour cream dressing.

*Or apple juice.

LAYERED WESTERN FRUIT MOLD

Yield: 48 portions

Ingredients

GELATIN, LEMON	1 24-ounce package
WATER, hot	2¼ quarts
WATER, cold	1½ quarts
LEMON JUICE	1 cup
SALT	1½ teaspoons
RIPE OLIVES, cut in wedges	3 cups
CELERY, chopped	3 cups
GRAPEFRUIT SECTIONS, FRESH	3 cups
CREAM CHEESE	1 pound

Procedure

1. Dissolve gelatin in hot water. Add cold water, lemon juice and salt.

2. Chill 1½ quarts of the mixture until thick enough to mound on a spoon. Fold in ripe olives, celery and grapefruit.

3. Turn into two 20-inch by 12-inch by 2-inch pans. Chill.

4. Whip cream cheese with remaining gelatin until well blended. Chill until mixture thickens and mounds on a spoon.

5. Turn into pans on top of almost-firm layer. Chill until firm.

6. Cut into portions. Serve on salad greens. Garnish with whole ripe olives, if desired.

CRANBERRY PINEAPPLE SALAD

Yield: 50 ½-cup portions

Ingredients

GELATIN, ORANGE	1-1/2 pounds
SALT	1/2 teaspoon
WATER, hot	3 quarts
CRANBERRIES, FRESH, RAW	2 pounds
ORANGES, including skins	1 pound
PINEAPPLE, CANNED, crushed,	
including juice	1-3/4 pounds
SUGAR	2 pounds
CELERY, diced	6 ounces
NUTS, chopped	6 ounces

Procedure

1. Dissolve gelatin and salt in hot water.
2. Chill until slightly thickened.
3. Grind raw cranberries and oranges. Mix with pineapple, sugar, celery and nuts.
4. Fold fruit mixture into gelatin. Pour into shallow pans or individual molds.
5. Chill until firm. Cut into squares or unmold. Serve on crisp greens.

ARABIAN PEACH MOLD ⟶

Yield: 42 3-ounce portions

Ingredients

PEACHES, CANNED, sliced,	
juice included	1-3/4 quarts
WHOLE CLOVES	1-1/2 tablespoons
STICK CINNAMON	1-1/2 ounces
VINEGAR	1-1/2 cups
SUGAR	3 cups
GELATIN, ORANGE	1 pound (2-1/3 cups)

STRAWBERRY SEAFOAM SALAD

Yield: 48 portions

Ingredients

STRAWBERRIES, sliced, frozen, thawed	6-1/2 pounds
PEAR HALVES	1 No. 10 can
STRAWBERRY AND PEAR SYRUP	1-1/2 quarts
GELATIN, LEMON	1-1/2 pounds
CREAM CHEESE	2-1/4 pounds
MILK	3/4 cup
CREAM, HEAVY (for whipping)	3 cups

Procedure

1. Drain strawberries, reserving syrup.

2. Drain pears, reserving syrup. Add enough pear syrup to strawberry syrup to make required amount. Put pears through food mill or sieve.

3. Heat syrup mixture just to boiling; dissolve gelatin.

4. Blend cheese and milk; beat in gelatin mixture. Chill until slightly thickened.

5. Whip cream.

6. Fold strawberries and sieved pears into the gelatin mixture. Fold in whipped cream.

7. Turn into individual molds, buffet molds or 12-inch by 20-inch by 2-inch pans. Chill until firm.

8. Unmold or cut into squares. Serve on crisp greens.

Procedure

1. Drain peaches. Tie cloves in small cheesecloth bag.

2. Combine juice, spices, vinegar and sugar. Bring to a boil. Add peaches, cover, simmer 10 minutes.

3. Drain peaches; remove spices. Measure syrup and add hot water to make 2¾ quarts.

4. Dissolve gelatin in hot liquid. Chill until slightly thickened; fold in peaches.

5. Turn into rectangular pans to a depth of 1¼ inches, or into molds. Chill until firm. Cut into squares or unmold. Serve on crisp lettuce or chicory.

SELF-LAYERED FRUIT SALAD

Yield: 35 portions

Ingredients

GELATIN, LIME	1½ pounds
WATER, boiling	2 quarts
WATER, very cold	1½ quarts
GRAPEFRUIT SECTIONS, CANNED, well drained	1 quart
DARK SWEET CHERRIES, CANNED, pitted, well drained	1 quart
NUTS, chopped	1 quart

Procedure

VERSION NO. 1

1. Dissolve gelatin in boiling water. Add cold water; mix.

2. Pour into a 12-inch by 18-inch by 2-inch pan. Add fruits and nuts; stir to distribute evenly.

3. Chill until firm. Cut into squares. Serve on crisp salad greens.

VERSION NO. 2

Use cherry gelatin; 1 quart drained canned sliced peaches; 1 quart drained canned pineapple tidbits; 1 quart sliced bananas.

VERSION NO. 3

Use raspberry gelatin; 1 quart drained canned pear halves, cut in half; 1 quart drained canned apricot halves; 1 quart diced raw apples.

VERSION NO. 4

Use orange gelatin; 2 quarts drained canned fruits for salad; 1 quart halved and seeded Tokay grapes.

LAYERED PRUNE SALAD

Yield: 48 portions

Ingredients

PRUNE JUICE	2½ quarts
LEMON JUICE	1 cup
SALT	2 teaspoons
GELATINE, UNFLAVORED	6 tablespoons
WATER, cold	1½ cups
PRUNES, cooked, pitted, chopped	1¼ quarts
CELERY, diced	2 cups
FRUIT COCKTAIL, drained	1 quart
GELATINE, UNFLAVORED	2 tablespoons
WATER, cold	1½ cups
COTTAGE CHEESE	3 quarts
PRUNES, whole cooked or plumped	48

Procedure

1. Combine prune juice, lemon juice and salt. Heat to boiling.
2. Soften gelatine in cold water. Dissolve in the hot liquid.
3. Chill until very slightly thickened. Fold in prunes, celery and fruit cocktail. Turn half of this mixture into two 9-inch by 16-inch by 2-inch pans. Chill until beginning to firm. Hold remainder of prune mixture, keeping it in the syrupy stage.
4. Soften second amount of gelatine in cold water. Dissolve over hot water. Stir into cottage cheese.
5. Spread cheese mixture over prune layer in pans.
6. Pour remainder of prune mixture over cheese, making the third layer. Refrigerate until firm.
7. Cut into squares. Serve on crisp salad greens. Garnish with mayonnaise and whole cooked prunes.

Dynamic Duo (Recipe, facing page)

Cling Peach Advisory Board and Western Iceberg Lettuce, Inc.

JELLIED ORANGE-GRAPEFRUIT-AVOCADO SALAD

Yield: 48 ½-cup portions

Ingredients

GELATIN, LEMON FLAVOR	1½ pounds
SALT	1½ teaspoons
WATER, hot	1 gallon
GRAPEFRUIT SECTIONS, cubed	1½ pounds (3 cups)
ORANGE SECTIONS, cubed	1¾ pounds (1 quart)
*AVOCADOS, cubed	2½ pounds (2 quarts)

Procedure

1. Dissolve gelatin and salt in hot water. Chill until mixture begins to thicken. Add grapefruit, orange and avocado.

2. Pour into individual molds or shallow pans. Chill until firm.

3. Unmold or cut into squares. Serve on crisp salad greens.

*Prepare avocado last and cover with citrus fruit mixture to avoid discoloration.

DYNAMIC DUO
(See picture, facing page)

Yield: 96 portions

Ingredients

FRUIT COCKTAIL	1 No. 10 can
GELATIN, LEMON	3 pounds
SALT	2 tablespoons
WATER, boiling	2 quarts
ICE WATER	3 quarts
SYRUP FROM FRUIT COCKTAIL	1 quart
VINEGAR	1 cup
LETTUCE, ICEBERG, shredded	2 pounds (1 gallon)
ONIONS, minced	1 cup
CELERY SEED	2 tablespoons
GELATIN, STRAWBERRY	3 pounds
WATER, boiling	2 quarts
ICE WATER	1 gallon
FROZEN STRAWBERRIES, sliced, sweetened, partially thawed	1 No. 10 can
LETTUCE, ICEBERG, separated as leaves	6 pounds
COTTAGE CHEESE, CREAMED, beaten	6 pounds

Procedure

1. Drain fruit cocktail, reserving required amount of syrup. Set aside drained fruit.

2. Dissolve lemon gelatin and salt in boiling water. Add ice water, measured syrup from fruit cocktail and vinegar. Chill until slightly thickened.

3. Add shredded lettuce, onion and celery seed; mix well. Divide gelatin mixture evenly into two 12-inch by 20-inch by 2½-inch pans. Chill until firm.

4. Dissolve strawberry gelatin in boiling water. Add ice water and strawberries.

5. Chill, if necessary, until slightly thickened. Add drained fruit cocktail. Divide evenly into two more 12-inch by 20-inch by 2½-inch pans. Chill until firm.

6. To serve, line salad plates with lettuce leaves. Cut each pan 16 by 3. Arrange 1 slice of each flavor, cut sides up, side by side on lettuce. Using pastry bag, pipe 1 ounce cottage cheese down center where slices meet. (Or, cut gelatin into cubes; pile the two flavors onto lettuce. Garnish with cottage cheese.)

CRANBERRY SALAD OR GARNISH

Yield: 24 portions

Ingredients

GELATIN, LEMON	12 ounces
WATER, hot	1¼ quarts
WHOLE CRANBERRY SAUCE	4 1-pound cans
WALNUTS, chopped	1 cup
BANANAS	6

Procedure

1. Dissolve gelatin in hot water. Stir in cranberry sauce. Chill until slightly thickened.

2. Add nuts and sliced bananas. Pour into individual molds or in a 16-inch by 10-inch by 2½-inch pan. Chill until firm. Serve as salad or cold plate garnish.

CHERRY COLA SALAD

Yield: 50 ½-cup portions

Ingredients

PEAR HALVES	1 No. 10 can
PEAR JUICE AND WATER	2 quarts
GELATIN, CHERRY	1½ pounds (3½ cups)
COLA FLAVORED CARBONATED BEVERAGE	2 quarts
CELERY, coarsely chopped	1 quart
WALNUTS, coarsely chopped	2 cups

Procedure

1. Drain pears, reserving juice. Add water to juice to make required amount of liquid. Bring to a boil.

2. Dissolve gelatin in the hot liquid. Cool slightly; add cola beverage. Chill until slightly thickened.

3. Dice pears. Fold pears, celery and walnuts into slightly thickened gelatin mixture.

4. Pour into individual molds or shallow pans. Chill until firm.

5. Unmold or cut into squares. Serve on crisp salad greens. Serve with a sour cream or whipped cream dressing.

JELLIED LIME, PINEAPPLE AND CHEESE SALAD

Yield: 96 portions

Ingredients

GELATIN, LIME	2¼ pounds
WATER, hot	2 quarts
PINEAPPLE CHUNKS	1 No. 10 can
PINEAPPLE SYRUP, drained from chunks	3¾ cups
PINEAPPLE JUICE	1 No. 10 can
CELERY, finely sliced	4 pounds (1 gallon)
AMERICAN CHEESE, shredded	2 pounds

Procedure

1. Dissolve gelatin in hot water.
2. Drain pineapple chunks, reserving syrup.
3. Add pineapple syrup and pineapple juice to gelatin. Chill until slightly thickened.
4. Fold drained pineapple, celery and cheese into gelatin; mix gently.
5. Pour into four 12-inch by 20-inch by 2-inch pans. Chill until firm.
6. Cut into squares; serve on crisp salad greens.

TRIPLE TREAT SALAD

Yield: 108 portions

Ingredients

GELATIN, ORANGE	1½ pounds
GELATIN, STRAWBERRY	1½ pounds
GELATIN, RASPBERRY	1½ pounds
WATER, boiling	1½ gallons
WATER, cold	1½ gallons
PEACHES, CANNED, sliced drained	3 quarts
BING CHERRIES, CANNED, pitted, drained	1½ quarts

Procedure

1. Mix the three flavors of gelatin; dissolve in boiling water, stirring until completely dissolved. Add cold water.
2. Chill until slightly thickened; add peaches and cherries. Pour into shallow pans. Chill until firm.
3. Cut into squares; serve on crisp salad greens.

MINTED MELON SALAD

Yield: 32 4-ounce portions

Ingredients

GELATIN, LIME FLAVOR	2-1/3 cups
SALT	1 teaspoon
FRESH MINT, chopped	1/2 cup (lightly packed)
WATER, hot	2-3/4 quarts
HONEYDEW MELON BALLS OR CUBES	2 quarts

Procedure

1. Combine gelatin, salt and mint. Add hot water; stir until gelatin is dissolved.
2. Let stand ten minutes; strain through cheesecloth.
3. Chill until slightly thickened; fold in the melon.
4. Turn into individual molds; chill until firm.
5. Unmold on crisp salad greens. Serve garnished with mayonnaise and sour cream dressing.

FRUITED CIDER SALAD

Yield: 32 portions

Ingredients

GELATIN, ORANGE	1 pound (2-1/3 cups)
SALT	1/2 teaspoon
CIDER OR APPLE JUICE, hot	2 quarts
WATER, hot	2 cups
APRICOT HALVES, CANNED, drained, quartered	3 cups
BANANAS, sliced	1 quart
CELERY, thinly sliced	2 cups

Procedure

1. Dissolve gelatin and salt in hot liquid. Chill until slightly thickened.
2. Fold in apricots, bananas and celery.
3. Turn into individual molds or shallow pans. Chill until firm.
4. Unmold or cut into squares. Serve on crisp salad greens.

Note

Excellent served with baked ham.

UNDER-THE-SEA SALAD

Yield: 32 4-ounce portions

Ingredients

CANNED PEAR SYRUP AND WATER	1-3/4 quarts
GELATIN, LIME	12 ounces (1-3/4 cups)
SALT	1 teaspoon
VINEGAR	2 tablespoons
GINGER, ground	1/2 teaspoon
CREAM CHEESE, softened	2-1/2 cups
PEARS, CANNED, drained, diced	1 quart

Procedure

1. Heat pear syrup and water.
2. Dissolve gelatin and salt in hot liquid. Add vinegar.
3. Pour half of mixture into individual molds, filling one-fourth full. Chill until firm.
4. Chill remaining gelatin mixture until slightly thickened. Turn into mixer bowl; whip at medium speed 15 to 20 minutes or until mixture has doubled in bulk and is fluffy and thick.
5. Add ginger to cheese; blend thoroughly.
6. Fold cheese mixture into whipped gelatin. Fold in pears.
7. Spread over firm gelatin in molds. Chill until firm.
8. Unmold. Serve on crisp salad greens.

JELLIED WALDORF SALAD

Yield: 48 ½-cup portions

Ingredients

GELATIN, LEMON	1-1/2 pounds
WATER, hot	1 gallon
APPLES, RED SKINNED, diced	2-1/2 pounds (2-1/2 quarts)
CELERY, diced	1 pound (1 quart)
NUTS, chopped	1/2 pound (8 ounces)

Procedure

1. Dissolve gelatin in hot water. Chill until slightly thickened.
2. Fold apples, celery and nuts into slightly thickened gelatin. Pour into individual molds or shallow pans. Chill until firm.
3. Unmold or cut into squares. Serve on crisp salad greens.

RIBBON MOLD SALAD

Yield: 40 portions, 1¾-inch slice each

Ingredients

GELATIN, LIME	1½ cups
WATER, hot	1½ quarts
GRAPES, halved, seeded	1½ pounds
GELATIN, LEMON	1 cup
WATER, hot	2 cups
PINEAPPLE JUICE, CANNED	2 cups
CREAM CHEESE	1 pound
MAYONNAISE	3 cups
GELATIN, RASPBERRY	1½ cups
WATER, hot	1½ quarts
BANANAS, sliced	4

Procedure

1. Dissolve lime gelatin in hot water. Chill until slightly thickened; add grapes. Pour into four 8½-inch by 4½-inch by 2½-inch loaf pans. Chill until firm.

2. Dissolve lemon gelatin in hot water. Add the pineapple juice. Chill until slightly thickened. Beat until fluffy. Blend cream cheese with mayonnaise. Fold into the whipped gelatin. Pour in pans on top of the layer of lime gelatin. Chill until firm.

3. Dissolve raspberry gelatin in hot water. Chill until slightly thickened. Fold in the sliced bananas. Pour in pans over the lemon gelatin and cream cheese layer. Chill until firm.

4. To serve: unmold and cut in 1¾-inch slices. Serve on a bed of shredded lettuce; garnish with creamy mayonnaise.

CHERRY AND ALMOND MOLDED SALAD

Yield: 48 portions

Ingredients

DARK SWEET CHERRIES, CANNED, pitted, drained	1 quart
GELATIN, CHERRY	1½ pounds
WATER, boiling	2 quarts
SYRUP FROM CHERRIES AND WATER, cold	2 quarts
LEMON JUICE	1 cup
ALMONDS, slivered	2 cups
CELERY, diced	1 quart
CREAM CHEESE	2 pounds
MILK OR CREAM	as needed
RED FOOD COLORING	as needed

Procedure

1. Drain sufficient canned, pitted dark sweet cherries to give required amount of drained fruit. Measure syrup; add water to make up required amount of cold liquid.

2. Dissolve gelatin in boiling water. Add cold syrup mixture and lemon juice. Chill until slightly thickened.

3. Fold drained cherries, almonds and celery into gelatin. Turn into individual molds. Chill until firm.

4. Soften cream cheese with a small amount of milk or cream. Tint mixture a delicate pink.

5. Unmold gelatin onto crisp greens. Using a pastry bag with a star tube, garnish each salad with a rosette of the cheese mixture.

AVOCADO SALAD

Yield: 1½ gallons, 48 ½-cup portions

Ingredients

GELATIN, LIME	1½ pounds
WATER, hot	3½ quarts
MAYONNAISE	3 cups
AVOCADOS, diced	2¼ quarts
LIME OR LEMON JUICE	1½ cups
SALT	1½ tablespoons
ONION, finely grated	1 tablespoon

Procedure

1. Dissolve gelatin in hot water. Cool.

2. Gradually add mayonnaise, blending with a whip. Chill until slightly thickened.

3. Combine avocado, lime juice, salt and onion; marinate 15 minutes.

4. Fold avocado mixture into slightly thickened gelatin. Pour into individual molds or shallow pans. Chill until firm.

5. Unmold or cut into squares. Serve on crisp greens.

BLACKBERRY FRUIT SALAD
(Self-Layering)

Yield: 40 portions

Ingredients

GELATIN, BLACKBERRY	1½ pounds
WATER, boiling	2 quarts
WATER, cold	2 quarts
GREEN GRAPES	1 quart
BANANAS, sliced	1 quart

Procedure

1. Dissolve gelatin in boiling water; stir until completely dissolved. Add cold water.

2. Pour into shallow pans. Add grapes and bananas. To prevent darkening be sure that each slice of banana is coated with gelatin. (As the gelatin sets, fruit will layer, grapes will go to the bottom, bananas on top.) Chill until firm.

3. Cut into squares; serve on crisp salad greens.

CINNAMON APPLE SALAD

Yield: 48 portions

Ingredients

RED HOTS (small, red, cinnamon candies)	3 cups
WATER, hot	3 quarts
GELATIN, LEMON	1-1/2 packages (36 ounces)
APPLESAUCE, unsweetened	3 quarts
CREAM CHEESE	36 ounces
COFFEE CREAM	1-1/2 cups
MAYONNAISE	3/4 cup

Procedure

1. Dissolve red hots in 1 quart of the hot water.
2. Dissolve gelatin in remaining 2 quarts hot water. Combine liquid mixtures.
3. Add applesauce; pour into pans. Let cool until slightly thickened.
4. Mix cream cheese with cream and mayonnaise. *Swirl* through applesauce mixture and continue to set.
5. Cut into squares. Serve on lettuce leaf lined plate.

GINGERALE FRUIT SALAD

Yield: 32 4-ounce portions

Ingredients

GELATIN, LEMON OR STRAWBERRY	1 pound (2-1/3 cups)
SALT	1 teaspoon
WATER, boiling	3 cups
GINGERALE	2 quarts
CELERY, chopped	2 cups
PECANS, coarsely chopped	2 cups
FRUIT COCKTAIL, CANNED, drained	1-1/4 quarts
CRYSTALLIZED GINGER, finely cut	1/2 cup

Procedure

1. Dissolve gelatin and salt in boiling water. (If gelatin does not completely dissolve, place bowl over boiling water and stir until dissolved.)
2. Cool slightly. Add gingerale; chill until slightly thickened.
3. Fold in celery, pecans, drained fruit and ginger.
4. Turn into individual molds or shallow pans. Chill until firm.
5. Unmold or cut into squares. Serve on crisp salad greens.

The Entree Salad

Western Growers Assn.

MAIN DISH SALADS

THE IDEA of main dish salads is far from new but their popularity has been flourishing during recent years. And little wonder! An attractive luncheon offering that's adequately satisfying yet sparing of calories meets one of the urgent needs of this energy-sparing, push button age.

There's a wide variety among the hearty salads that fit this pattern. In addition to chef's salad bowls, fruit salad plates and cooked vegetable salads of ample proportions, there's the long line of salad mixtures comprised of meat, poultry, seafood, and similar ingredients in partnership with neatly cut crisp vegetables or pieces of fruit.

Salads of this type can be temptingly arranged on greens, using either a plate or a salad bowl. You can achieve variation with change-abouts in greens. Experiment with romaine, escarole, chicory and cress as well as all of the different varieties of lettuce.

Oval or leaf-shaped plates are a nice conceit. And salad bowls in soft, pretty colors can give an extra plus to these salads' good looks. For other presentations to catch the eye, try spooning the mixture into a cream puff shell. Or, use it to stuff red ripe tomatoes and to fill avocado halves or individual pastry shells.

CRAB LOUIS

Yield: 1 portion

Ingredients

LETTUCE CUPS, paprika edged	3
LETTUCE, shredded	1 cup
CRABMEAT	½ cup
*LOUIS DRESSING	½ cup
CRABLEGS	3
CHICORY	as needed
TOMATO WEDGES	3
EGG WEDGES	2
OLIVE, RIPE	1
OLIVE, GREEN	1
LEMON WEDGE	1

Procedure

1. Arrange lettuce cups along one side of an oval platter; fill with shredded lettuce.

2. Arrange crabmeat over lettuce; cover with dressing. Sprinkle dressing with paprika; top with crablegs.

3. Garnish plate with chicory topped with tomato and egg wedges. Serve with olives and lemon.

*LOUIS DRESSING

Yield: 3 gallons

Ingredients

CHILI SAUCE	1/2 gallon
SWEET PICKLE RELISH	1/3 gallon
ONIONS, chopped	2 large
PEPPER	4 teaspoons
MONOSODIUM GLUTAMATE	1 teaspoon
SUGAR	1 pound
MAYONNAISE	1 gallon
SALAD DRESSING	1 gallon
EGGS, hard-cooked, chopped	16

Procedure

1. Add chili sauce, relish, onion, pepper, monosodium glutamate and sugar to the mayonnaise and dressing. Mix well. Fold in eggs. Store in refrigerator.

SAVORY FISH SALAD

Yield: 100 portions

Ingredients

BOSTON BLUEFISH (POLLOCK)	
or OTHER FISH FILLETS,	
fresh or frozen	15 pounds
FRENCH DRESSING	1 quart
LEMON JUICE or VINEGAR	1 cup
SALAD OIL	½ cup
SOY SAUCE	1 tablespoon
DILL WEED	1 tablespoon
CELERY, diced	6 pounds
GREEN PEPPERS, diced	½ pound
EGGS, hard-cooked, chopped	24
PEAS, cooked	2 pounds
SWEET PICKLE RELISH, drained	1 cup
SALT	1 tablespoon
PEPPER	½ teaspoon
LEMON JUICE	½ cup
LIQUID HOT PEPPER SEASONING	several dashes
MAYONNAISE	1½ quarts

Procedure

1. Thaw fish.
2. Poach until fork tender in water to cover. Drain.
3. Combine French dressing, lemon juice, salad oil, soy sauce and dill weed. Pour over hot, drained fish. Let stand until cool. Refrigerate for several hours, turning fish several times.
4. Cube cold, marinated fillets. Combine with celery, green pepper, eggs and peas.
5. Blend pickle relish, salt, pepper, lemon juice and hot pepper seasoning with mayonnaise. Pour over salad ingredients; toss to mix.
6. Serve on crisp salad greens. Garnish as desired.

CREOLE SHRIMP SALAD NEW ORLEANS

Yield: 36 7-ounce portions

Ingredients

SHRIMP, cooked, shelled, cut in uniform pieces	4½ pounds (3¾ quarts)
RICE, cooked	2 quarts
CAULIFLOWER, raw, diced	2 quarts
GREEN PEPPERS, slivered	2 cups
PIMIENTOES, diced	2 cups
GREEN ONIONS (SCALLIONS), chopped	¾ cup
SALT	3 tablespoons
PEPPER	¾ teaspoon
MONOSODIUM GLUTAMATE	1 tablespoon
RIPE OLIVES, finely chopped	¾ cup
MAYONNAISE	3 cups
LETTUCE	as needed
WATERCRESS	as needed
RIPE OLIVE SLICES	as needed
GREEN ONIONS	72 (2 per serving)

Procedure

1. Combine shrimp, rice, cauliflower, green peppers, pimientoes and chopped scallions; mix lightly.

2. Add seasonings and ripe olives to mayonnaise. Pour over salad mixture; toss together lightly. Taste and correct seasonings.

3. Portion salad into crisp lettuce cups. Garnish with a spray of watercress and a few olive slices. Place 2 green onions at side of plate.

MARINATED SHRIMP SALAD

Yield: 24 portions

Ingredients

SALT	1-1/2 tablespoons
WHOLE BLACK PEPPER	12 peppercorns
MUSTARD, DRY	1-1/2 tablespoons
SUGAR	1 tablespoon
DILL WEED	1 tablespoon
SCALLIONS, minced	2 tablespoons
LEMON JUICE	1/4 cup
BEER or ALE	1-1/2 quarts
SHRIMP, RAW	5 pounds
CELERY, diced	1-1/4 quarts
MAYONNAISE	3 cups
MARINADE (reserved)	1/3 cup

Procedure

1. Combine salt, pepper, mustard, sugar, dill weed, scallions, lemon juice and beer.

2. Bring to a boil; simmer 1 minute.

3. Add shrimp; return to a boil; simmer 3 minutes or until shrimp turn pink. Cool shrimp in liquid.

4. Remove required amount of marinade; set aside.

5. Shell shrimp; de-vein. Use remaining marinade to rinse shrimp; drain.

6. Combine shrimp, celery, mayonnaise and reserved marinade. Toss to mix. Chill.

7. Serve on crisp salad greens allowing ½ cup per portion.

AVOCADO DILLED SHRIMP SALAD

Yield: 24 portions

Ingredients

SALAD OIL	2 cups
WHITE WINE VINEGAR	1 cup
DILL WEED	1 tablespoon
SALT	1 tablespoon
SEASONED PEPPER	1 teaspoon
GARLIC, mashed	1 clove
SHRIMP, large, cooked, shelled deveined	72 (about 1½ pounds)
AVOCADOS, large	12
LEMON JUICE	as needed

Procedure

1. Combine oil, vinegar, seasonings and garlic.
2. Pour over shrimp; marinate in refrigerator at least 8 hours.
3. Cut avocados in half; remove seeds. Brush cavities with lemon juice.
4. Arrange 3 shrimp in each avocado half. Drizzle with a small amount of the marinade.
5. Serve as salad or appetizer.

SHRIMP SALAD

Yield: 25 portions (No. 16 scoop)

Ingredients

SHRIMP, peeled, deveined	6 pounds
CELERY, thinly sliced	1 quart
ONION, grated	1 small
PICKLE RELISH	½ cup
SALT	1 tablespoon
WHITE PEPPER	½ teaspoon
MONOSODIUM GLUTAMATE	1 teaspoon
MAYONNAISE	1½ cups

Procedure

1. Boil shrimp; cool; cut coarsely.
2. Combine all ingredients, tossing lightly. For full flavor, allow to set in refrigerator about 15 minutes before serving.

Service Styled for Shrimp

International Shrimp Council

PINEAPPLE SHRIMP SALAD

Yield: 48 portions

Ingredients

SHRIMP, cooked, deveined	12 pounds
PINEAPPLE TIDBITS, drained	1 No. 10 can
CELERY, finely chopped	1½ pounds
GREEN ONIONS, finely chopped	1 pound
COCONUT, FLAKED	8 ounces
CURRY POWDER	1 tablespoon
LEMON JUICE	1 cup
MAYONNAISE	1 cup
ROMAINE	as needed
LIME WEDGES	48
PINEAPPLE TIDBITS	48

Procedure

1. Combine shrimp, first amount of pineapple, celery, onions and coconut.

2. Blend curry powder and lemon juice with mayonnaise. Pour over shrimp mixture; mix lightly but well. Add more mayonnaise, if necessary, to hold ingredients together.

3. Spoon mixture into large sherbet glasses. Garnish with romaine and lime wedge. Top with skewered pineapple tidbits.

AVOCADO AND SALMON SALAD

Yield: 25 3½-ounce portions

Ingredients

AVOCADOS diced	1 quart
SALMON, flaked	1 quart
ONIONS, minced	1 cup
CELERY, chopped fine	1 cup
MAYONNAISE	1½ cups
LEMON JUICE	¼ cup
SALT	as needed
PEPPER, WHITE	½ teaspoon

Procedure

1. Combine all ingredients, tossing lightly to mix. Serve in lettuce cups; garnish with ripe olives and radish roses.

STUFFED AVOCADO SALAD

Yield: 24 portions

Ingredients

*TUNA, flaked	1 quart
CELERY, chopped	1 quart
MAYONNAISE	1 cup
LEMON JUICE	¼ cup
SALT	as needed
PEPPER	as needed
AVOCADOS, medium	12
SALAD GREENS	

Procedure

1. Combine flaked tuna and celery.

2. Blend mayonnaise and lemon juice; add salt and pepper. Pour over tuna mixture; mix lightly.

3. Cut each avocado in half lengthwise; remove seed and skin. Sprinkle with additional lemon juice and salt.

4. Arrange avocado halves on salad greens. Fill with salad mixture. Garnish with a strip of green pepper or pimiento, ripe olives and a sprig of parsley.

*Crab; diced lobster or diced chicken may be used.

SCALLOP SALAD, SAUCE VERTE

Yield: 20 portions

Ingredients

SCALLOPS, fresh or frozen	5 pounds
WATER, boiling	as needed
MAYONNAISE	1¼ quarts
CHIVES, chopped	½ cup
TARRAGON, DRY	1 tablespoon
PARSLEY, minced	½ cup
DILL WEED	1 tablespoon

Procedure

1. Defrost frozen scallops. Slice; rinse; dry.

2. Pour boiling water over scallops. Let stand 5 minutes or until scallops lose their transparency. Do not cook or boil. Drain. Chill.

3. Combine remaining ingredients; blend. Pour over scallops; mix gently.

4. Serve on lettuce. Garnish with tomato wedges, if desired.

ROCK LOBSTER SALAD

Yield: 25 1-cup portions

Ingredients

SOUTH AFRICAN ROCK LOBSTER TAILS	5 pounds
HARD-COOKED EGGS, diced	12
CELERY, diced	2 quarts
CUCUMBERS, diced	1 quart
SALT	2½ tablespoons
PEPPER	½ teaspoon
MAYONNAISE	1¼ cups

Procedure

1. Drop frozen lobster tails into boiling salted water. When water re-boils cook 3 minutes more than weight of individual tails in ounces. (For example, cook 5-ounce tails for 8 minutes.) Drain immediately; drench with cold water.

2. Remove lobster meat from shells; dice.

3. Toss lobster meat, eggs, celery, cucumber and seasonings together with mayonnaise. Chill thoroughly. Serve on crisp salad greens.

Anchovy Garnish for Vegetable Salad

Western Growers Assn.

TUNA-SHRIMP SALAD WITH LIME DRESSING

Yield: 25 portions

Ingredients

CATSUP	2 cups
WORCESTERSHIRE SAUCE	1 teaspoon
LIME RIND, grated	1 teaspoon
SALT	½ teaspoon
LIME JUICE	1 cup
DRY WHITE WINE	½ cup
TUNA FISH, drained	3½ pounds
SHRIMP, cooked	3 pounds
LETTUCE, shredded	2 to 3 heads
LIME WEDGES	25

Procedure

1. Combine catsup, Worcestershire, lime rind, salt, lime juice and wine.
2. Add tuna and shrimp. Mix lightly but thoroughly. Chill.
3. Serve on shredded lettuce. Garnish with lime wedges.

COTTAGE CHEESE AND SALMON SALAD

Yield: 50 ½-cup portions

Ingredients

SWEET PICKLES, chopped	3½ cups
SALAD DRESSING	3½ cups
COTTAGE CHEESE	3½ pounds
SALMON, flaked	7 1-pound cans
CELERY, chopped	3½ cups

Procedure

1. Mix pickles and salad dressing. Combine with remaining ingredients tossing lightly to mix.
2. Serve on crisp salad greens portioning with a No. 10 scoop. Garnish with a radish rose, lemon wedge, sweet pickle or sieved egg yolk.

FISHERMAN'S SALAD

Yield: 8 pounds

Ingredients

RED SALMON, fresh cooked, or canned, flaked	1 quart
CABBAGE, shredded	1 quart
EGGS, hard-cooked, chopped	18
POTATOES, cooked, diced	1 quart
SALT	1 tablespoon
LEMON JUICE	1½ tablespoons
WORCESTERSHIRE SAUCE	¼ cup
MAYONNAISE	2½ cups
TOMATO WEDGES	to garnish

Procedure

1. Combine the salmon, cabbage, eggs and potatoes; toss together lightly with two forks.

2. Add salt, lemon juice and Worcestershire sauce to mayonnaise; blend well.

3. Pour dressing over salad mixture. Toss lightly to mix. Chill.

4. Serve on lettuce; garnish with tomato wedge.

CURRIED SHRIMP SALAD ➤

Yield: 24 portions

Ingredients

SHRIMP, cooked, cut in pieces	3 quarts
CELERY, diced	1 quart
ONIONS, grated	1/4 cup
MAYONNAISE	3 cups
LEMON JUICE	1/3 cup
SALT	1-1/2 tablespoons
CURRY POWDER	3 to 4 tablespoons
SOUR CREAM	1 cup
COCONUT, FLAKED	1-3/4 cups

TUNA-RICE SALAD VALENCIANA

Yield: 12 portions

Ingredients

RICE, cooked	1¼ quarts
TUNA FISH, flaked	1 pound
CELERY, sliced	2 cups
OLIVES, stuffed, sliced	½ cup
DILL PICKLES, chopped	½ cup
MAYONNAISE	1¼ cups
CHILI SAUCE	¼ cup
LEMON JUICE	2 tablespoons
SALT	as needed
PEPPER	as needed
CAPERS (optional)	3 to 4 tablespoons

Procedure

1. Combine rice, tuna fish, celery, olives and pickles.

2. Combine mayonnaise, chili sauce and lemon juice. Pour over salad ingredients; toss lightly to mix. Check seasoning, adding salt and pepper as desired. Chill.

3. Serve on crisp salad greens. Garnish with capers.

Procedure

1. Combine shrimp and celery.

2. Combine grated onion, mayonnaise, lemon juice, salt and curry powder; mix thoroughly. Fold in sour cream, blending well.

3. Pour dressing over shrimp mixture; toss lightly to mix.

4. Serve on crisp salad greens allowing ¾ cup per portion. Sprinkle with coconut.

Serve a Turkey Salad Loaf

American Spice Trade Assn.

CHICKEN FRUIT SALAD SUPREME

Yield: 3 gallons

Ingredients

CHICKEN, cooked, diced	7½ pounds
	(1½ gallons)
FROZEN CONCENTRATE FOR IMITATION	
ORANGE JUICE*	2 cups
PINEAPPLE JUICE	2 cups
LEMON JUICE	1 cup
GRAPES, DARK, halved, seeded	4 pounds (1¾ quarts)
CELERY, diced	2 quarts
PINEAPPLE CHUNKS, drained	1¾ quarts
MAYONNAISE	1¾ quarts
MARINADE	2 cups
SOY SAUCE (optional)	½ cup
ALMONDS, slivered, toasted (optional)	1¾ quarts

Procedure

1. Season chicken with salt and pepper, if necessary.

2. Combine the concentrate, pineapple juice and lemon juice. Pour over chicken; toss lightly. Marinate 3 hours in refrigerator.

3. Drain chicken, reserving required amount of marinade. Add grapes, celery, pineapple, mayonnaise, reserved marinade, soy sauce and almonds. Toss lightly.

4. Serve on crisp salad greens.

*Or an equal measure of frozen orange juice concentrate.

TURKEY AND BEAN SALAD

Yield: 100 ½-cup portions

Ingredients

TURKEY or CHICKEN, cooked, coarsely chopped	4-1/2 pounds (3-1/2 quarts)
DRY BEANS, cooked*	5 quarts
SWEET PICKLE, coarsely chopped	2 quarts
CELERY, coarsely chopped	2-1/2 quarts
ONIONS, chopped	1-1/3 cups
EGGS, hard-cooked, diced	1-1/2 quarts
MAYONNAISE	3 cups
SALT	1/3 cup
MUSTARD, prepared	1/3 cup
PICKLE LIQUID	1/3 cup

Procedure

1. Combine turkey, beans, pickle, celery, onions and eggs.
2. Blend mayonnaise, salt, mustard and pickle juice. Pour over salad ingredients; toss lightly to mix.
3. Refrigerate 1 hour to blend flavors. Serve on crisp salad greens.

*Kidney, pinto, large lima or Great Northern beans.

TURKEY-ASPARAGUS SALAD ⟶

Yield: 12 4-ounce portions

Ingredients

TURKEY, diced	1 pound, 14 ounces
LEMON JUICE	2 tablespoons
CELERY, finely diced	2 cups
ONION, minced	1/3 cup
BLACK PEPPER	1/8 teaspoon
MAYONNAISE	3/4 cup
ASPARAGUS SPEARS, cooked, chilled	48 to 72
PIMIENTO STRIPS	12
HARD-COOKED EGGS, sliced	24 slices

CURRIED CHICKEN SALAD

Yield: 50 2/3-cup portions

Ingredients

RICE, uncooked	1 quart
ONIONS, minced	1¾ cups
VINEGAR	½ cup
SALAD OIL	1 cup
CURRY POWDER	2 tablespoons
CHICKEN, cooked, cubed	3½ quarts
CELERY, chopped	1¾ quarts
GREEN PEPPERS, chopped	1¾ cups
SALAD DRESSING	4½ cups
SALT	1 tablespoon

Procedure

1. Cook rice according to package directions. Cool thoroughly.

2. Combine rice, onion, vinegar, oil and curry powder; refrigerate several hours or overnight.

3. Combine chicken, rice mixture, celery, green peppers, salad dressing and salt; toss together lightly.

4. Serve on crisp salad greens.

Procedure

1. Sprinkle turkey with lemon juice. Chill several hours to develop flavor.

2. Place celery on top of turkey in bowl.

3. Add onion and pepper to mayonnaise; blend. Pour over celery and turkey. Toss lightly to mix.

4. Arrange 4 to 6 asparagus spears on crisp salad greens. Top with a portion of turkey salad. Garnish with pimiento strip and slices of hard cooked egg.

CALIFORNIA CHICKEN SALAD

Yield: 6 quarts

Ingredients

CHICKEN MEAT, diced	3¾ pounds
SALT	2 teaspoons
PEPPER, WHITE	1 teaspoon
ORANGE JUICE	1 cup
PINEAPPLE JUICE, unsweetened	1 cup
LEMON JUICE	½ cup
GRAPES, THOMPSON SEEDLESS	1 pound
GRAPES, RIBIER	1 pound
CELERY, diced	1 pound
ALMONDS, blanched, slivered	14 ounces
MAYONNAISE	1¾ pounds
MARINADE	1 cup

Procedure

1. Season chicken with salt and pepper. Add orange, pineapple and lemon juices; toss lightly. Refrigerate; marinate 3 hours.

2. Drain chicken well; reserve required amount of marinade.

3. Cut seedless grapes in half. Cut Ribier grapes in half; remove seeds.

4. Combine chicken, grapes, celery, almonds, mayonnaise and marinade; toss lightly. Chill.

5. Serve on crisp salad greens.

SAVORY EGG SALAD   ⟶

Yield: 50 2/3-cup portions

Ingredients

EGGS	8-1/3 dozen
PASCAL CELERY, cut in 1/4-inch pieces	2 quarts
STUFFED OLIVES, sliced	3 cups
ONIONS, minced	1-1/4 cups
SALAD DRESSING	3 cups
PREPARED MUSTARD	1/3 cup
SALT	3 tablespoons
PEPPER	1 teaspoon
SAVORY, rubbed	1-1/2 teaspoons

CHICKEN VEGETABLE SALAD

Yield: 2 gallons 50 5/8-cup portions

Ingredients

MAYONNAISE	1½ quarts
LEMON JUICE	2 tablespoons
PIMIENTOES, diced	¾ cup
SALT	2½ tablespoons
PEPPER	1½ teaspoons
RICE, cooked, cooled	2¼ quarts
PEAS, canned, drained	2½ quarts
CHICKEN, cooked, diced	2¼ quarts
CELERY, diced	2¼ quarts
SALAD GREENS	as needed
TOMATO WEDGES	100
ASPARAGUS TIPS, marinated	50

Procedure

1. Mix mayonnaise, lemon juice, pimiento and seasonings.

2. Add cooked rice, peas, chicken and celery to mayonnaise mixture; toss together lightly. Chill about 1 hour before serving.

3. Serve a No. 8 scoop on salad greens. Arrange a tomato wedge, rounded side up, at each side of mound. Place an asparagus tip across top of chicken parallel to tomato wedges.

Note

Crabmeat, lobster or shrimp may be substituted for the chicken.

Procedure

1. Cover eggs with cold water; bring to a boil. Cover the pot, turn off heat and allow eggs to stand in hot water 20 minutes. Drain; cover with cold water. Peel.

2. Chop all but 13 of the hard-cooked eggs. Combine with celery, olives and onion.

3. Blend salad dressing and seasonings; combine with egg mixture. Chill until ready for service.

4. Quarter the remaining eggs. For each portion, serve 2/3 cup salad on lettuce; garnish with one-quarter hard-cooked egg. (Crisp crumbled bacon pieces may be used as garnish, if desired.)

CHICKEN, EGG AND ALMOND SALAD IN PASTRY SHELLS

Yield: 48 portions

Ingredients

CHICKEN, cooked, diced	1 gallon
CELERY, chopped	1 quart
DICED EGGS	3 quarts
ALMONDS, roasted, diced	1 quart
MAYONNAISE	2 cups
SOUR CREAM	2 cups
LEMON JUICE	1 cup
SALT	1-1/2 tablespoons
PEPPER	1/2 teaspoon
MUSTARD, DRY	1 tablespoon
PASTRY TART SHELLS, baked	48
SOUR CREAM	2 cups
ALMONDS, roasted, diced	2 cups

Procedure

1. Combine chicken, celery, diced eggs and first amount of almonds.
2. Blend mayonnaise, first amount of sour cream, lemon juice and seasonings. Pour over chicken mixture; toss lightly to mix.
3. Fill each pastry shell with ½ cup of mixture.
4. Top with remaining sour cream; sprinkle with remaining almonds.

PINEAPPLE CHICKEN SALAD

Yield: 55 portions

Ingredients

CHICKEN, cooked, cubed	4-1/2 quarts
CELERY, sliced	1-1/2 quarts
SALT	2-1/3 tablespoons
LEMON JUICE	2 tablespoons
SALAD DRESSING	2-1/2 cups
PINEAPPLE TIDBITS, drained	1 No. 10 can
WALNUTS, chopped	2 cups

Procedure

1. Combine ingredients. Mix lightly. Chill. Serve on crisp salad greens.

Color Contrasts in Hearty Salad Bowl

Associated Blue Lake Green Bean Canners, Inc.

TURKEY SALAD

Yield: 24 portions

Ingredients

TURKEY ROLL, cut in ½-inch cubes	2½ pounds
FRENCH DRESSING, thin	½ cup
CELERY, sliced	2 quarts
GRAPES, halved, seeded	1 quart
SALT	2 teaspoons
PEPPER, WHITE	½ teaspoon
LEMON JUICE	2 teaspoons
MAYONNAISE	2½ cups
SOUR CREAM	1 cup
ALMONDS, slivered, toasted	1½ cups

Procedure

1. Toss diced turkey with French dressing. Let stand, refrigerated, 1 to 2 hours.

2. Add celery and grapes.

3. Combine salt, pepper and lemon juice with mayonnaise; fold in sour cream. Add dressing to turkey mixture; toss lightly to mix.

4. Serve on crisp salad greens. Sprinkle salad with almonds.

HAM AND FRESH ORANGE SALAD

Yield: 24 portions

Ingredients

MAYONNAISE	1 cup
HEAVY CREAM or SOUR CREAM	¼ cup
ONIONS, fresh, minced	¼ cup
LEMON JUICE	¼ cup
SALT	1 teaspoon
PEPPER, BLACK, ground	¼ teaspoon
HAM or LUNCHEON MEAT, diced	2 quarts
ORANGE SECTIONS	1½ quarts
CELERY, diced	1 quart
LETTUCE CUPS	as needed
WALNUTS, chopped	2 cups
WATERCRESS	as needed
ORANGE SECTIONS	3 cups

Procedure

1. Blend mayonnaise, cream, onions, lemon juice, salt and pepper.
2. Combine ham, first amount of orange sections and celery. Add mayonnaise mixture; toss lightly.
3. Portion on lettuce. Garnish with walnuts, watercress and orange sections.

FRUITED VEAL SALAD

Yield: 24 portions

Ingredients

VEAL, cooked, cubed	3 quarts
PINEAPPLE, chunks, drained	3 No. 303 cans
CELERY, diced	1½ quarts
EGGS, hard-cooked, diced	6
ALMONDS, salted	3 cups
MAYONNAISE	as needed

Procedure

1. Combine veal, pineapple, celery and eggs. Chill thoroughly.
2. Just before serving, add almonds and enough mayonnaise to moisten ingredients. Mix lightly. Serve on crisp salad greens.

FRANKFURTER SALAD

Yield: 48 ¾-cup portions

Ingredients

SALAD DRESSING	2 cups
CHILI SAUCE	1 cup
VINEGAR	3/4 cup
ONIONS, chopped	2 cups
MUSTARD, prepared	1/3 cup
SALT	1 tablespoon
FRANKFURTERS, cooked, sliced diagonally	6 pounds (4-1/2 quarts)
POTATOES, cooked, cubed	1 gallon
CUCUMBERS, chopped	1 quart

Procedure

1. Combine salad dressing, chili sauce, vinegar, onions, mustard and salt.

2. Toss dressing lightly with frankfurters, potatoes and cucumbers. Add salt to taste, if necessary. Chill.

3. Serve in lettuce cups; garnish with green pepper rings.

HAM AND PECAN SALAD

Yield: 60 1-cup portions

Ingredients

HAM, cooked, diced	12 pounds
CELERY, diced	6 pounds
PINEAPPLE, drained, diced	6 pounds
MAYONNAISE	1½ quarts
SALT	2 ounces
SUGAR, CONFECTIONERS'	1 pound 4 ounces
PECANS, chopped	2½ cups

Procedure

1. Dice ham into ¼-inch cubes. Add to celery and pineapple.

2. Combine mayonnaise, salt and sugar; blend. Pour over salad ingredients; mix lightly.

3. Serve on crisp salad greens. Top with chopped pecans.

CURRIED LAMB SALAD

Yield: 1½ gallons, 24 1-cup portions

Ingredients

LAMB, cooked, cut julienne	3 quarts
	(4 pounds)
COCONUT, chopped	2 cups
CELERY, thinly sliced	3 cups
ORANGES, peeled, cut lengthwise and sliced	12 medium
CURRY POWDER	2 tablespoons
SALT	2 tablespoons
PEPPER	¾ teaspoon
MAYONNAISE	2 cups

Procedure

1. Combine lamb, coconut, celery and oranges. Chill thoroughly.
2. Blend curry powder, salt and pepper with mayonnaise. Pour over chilled lamb mixture; toss lightly to mix.
3. Serve in lettuce cups. Garnish with additional orange slices, if desired.

HAM AND PINEAPPLE SALAD

Yield: 7½ quarts, 45 ¾-cup portions

Ingredients

PINEAPPLE TIDBITS, drained	1 No. 10 can
CELERY, diced	2 quarts
HAM, cooked, cubed	1½ quarts
PIMIENTOES, diced	1 cup
CREAM DRESSING (mayonnaise and sour cream)	2 quarts
SALT	1 tablespoon

Procedure

1. Combine pineapple, celery, ham and pimiento. Chill.
2. Blend dressing with salt. Just before serving, pour dressing over salad mixture; toss lightly to mix. Taste and season with more salt if necessary.
3. Serve on crisp salad greens. Garnish with pimiento rings and watercress.

HONOLULU SALAD

Yield: 25 5-ounce portions

Ingredients

MEAT, cooked, diced	1 quart
CELERY, diced	1 quart
SALT	1 tablespoon
PEPPER, WHITE	1 teaspoon
PAPRIKA	1 teaspoon
PARSLEY, chopped	¼ cup
FRENCH DRESSING	1 cup
PINEAPPLE RINGS	25
MAYONNAISE	2 cups

Procedure

1. Combine meat, celery, seasonings and French dressing; chill until flavors are blended.

2. Arrange pineapple in a lettuce cup or on shredded lettuce; top with a mound of salad.

3. Garnish with mayonnaise; sprinkle with paprika.

COUNTRY CLUB SALAD

Yield: 48 ¾-cup portions

Ingredients

HAM, CANNED	6¼ pounds
CARROTS, cooked, diced	1½ quarts
GREEN LIMA BEANS, cooked	2 quarts
CELERY, diced	1¼ quarts
ONIONS, minced	1½ cups
GREEN PEPPERS, diced	2½ cups
MAYONNAISE or SALAD DRESSING	1 quart
EGGS, hard-cooked	12

Procedure

1. Slice ham; dice in 3/8-inch cubes.

2. Toss together with vegetables and mayonnaise. Chill.

3. Serve on crisp salad greens. Garnish with a wedge of hard-cooked egg.

FRANKFURTER SALAD BOWL

Yield: 50 portions

Ingredients

KIDNEY BEANS, canned or cooked	1 gallon
FRANKFURTERS, sliced	4 to 6 pounds
SOUR PICKLES, sliced	1¼ quarts
FRENCH DRESSING	1 quart
ONIONS, thinly sliced	4
LETTUCE	as needed

Procedure

1. Drain kidney beans.
2. Add frankfurters, pickles, 2 cups French dressing, onions. Chill.
3. Add remaining French dressing. Serve on lettuce or in individual salad bowls lined with shredded lettuce.

ORANGE AND HAM RICE SALAD

Yield: 12 portions

Ingredients

RICE, cooked	1½ quarts
HAM, cooked, cut in julienne strips	2 cups
ONIONS, minced	2 tablespoons
GREEN PEPPERS, cut in julienne strips	1 cup
MANDARIN ORANGE SEGMENTS, drained	2 11-ounce cans
SOUR CREAM	2 cups
SALT	as needed
PEPPER, WHITE	as needed

Procedure

1. Combine rice, ham, onion, green pepper, orange segments and sour cream. Toss lightly to mix. Check seasoning, adding salt and pepper, as desired. Chill.
2. Serve on crisp salad greens.

Summer Serenade Salad

Heinz U. S. A., Div. of H. J. Heinz Co.

SUMMER SERENADE SALAD

Yield: 52 ½-cup portions

Ingredients

SALAD DRESSING	2 cups
CATSUP	¾ cup
VINEGAR	2 tablespoons
INSTANT ONIONS, finely rolled	1 tablespoon
RICE, cooked	3 quarts
PEAS, frozen, cooked	2 quarts
AMERICAN or PROCESS SHARP CHEESE, slivered	1 pound
HAM, cooked, diced	1½ pounds
DILL PICKLE RELISH, well-drained	1½ cups

Procedure

1. Combine salad dressing, catsup, vinegar and onions. Add to rice; toss to mix.
2. Add remaining ingredients; mix lightly but thoroughly.
3. Chill several hours to blend flavors.
4. Serve on crisp salad greens.

SPECIAL LUNCHEON SALAD

Yield: 50 ¾-cup portions

Ingredients

PORK SHOULDER, cooked, cubed	2 quarts*
VEAL SHOULDER, cooked, cubed	2 quarts*
FRENCH DRESSING	1 cup
APPLES, diced (leave red skins on)	2 quarts
CELERY, chopped	2 quarts
RIPE OLIVES, chopped	1½ cups
SALAD DRESSING	3 cups
LEMON JUICE	¼ cup
THYME	½ teaspoon
SALT	2 tablespoons

*7 pounds of pork shoulder and 7 pounds of veal shoulder will yield this amount.

To Cook Meat

Simmer meats together with 1 tablespoon salt and 1 tablespoon monosodium glutamate, approximately 4 hours or until meat is fork-tender, chill. Trim out fat and bone. Cut into cubes.

Procedure

1. Pour French dressing over meat. Mix thoroughly until each piece is coated. Let stand in refrigerator at least 2 hours to blend flavors.

2. Add apples, celery and olives to meat.

3. Combine salad dressing, lemon juice, thyme and salt. Pour over mixture. Stir lightly to blend. Chill.

4. Serve on crisp lettuce or other salad greens.

HAM SALAD WITH CAPERS ⟶

Yield: 4½ quarts

Ingredients

MAYONNAISE	3/4 cup
SOUR CREAM	1-1/3 cups
PEPPER	1/2 teaspoon
CAPERS	1/2 cup
HAM, fully cooked, cut in 1/2-inch cubes	4 pounds
CUCUMBERS, thinly sliced	3 cups
CELERY, finely diced	2 cups

SWEETBREAD CHICKEN SALAD

Yield: 25 ½-cup portions

Ingredients

MAYONNAISE	2 cups
SHERRY, DRY	1/3 cup
LEMON JUICE	1/3 cup
PARSLEY, chopped	1/3 cup
DILL, DRIED	1-1/2 teaspoons
SEASONED SALT	1 teaspoon
VEAL SWEETBREADS, precooked, cut into chunks	4 pair
CHICKEN, CANNED, boned, cut into chunks	1 quart
CELERY, sliced or chopped	1 quart
ONIONS, GREEN, sliced or chopped	2 cups
ALMONDS, slivered, toasted	3/4 cup
LETTUCE CUPS	25
WATERCRESS or PARSLEY	25 sprigs

Procedure

1. Combine mayonnaise, sherry, lemon juice ana seasonings; mix well.

2. Add sweetbreads, chicken, celery, onions and almonds; mix lightly, Chill.

3. Serve a No. 8 scoop of salad in lettuce cup. Garnish with watercress or parsley.

Procedure

1. Combine mayonnaise, sour cream, pepper and capers; blend.

2. Combine ham, cucumbers and celery. Add dressing; toss lightly to mix.

RIPE OLIVE CHEESE SALAD

Yield: 24 ½-cup portions

Ingredients

RIPE OLIVES,CANNED, pitted, drained	1½ quarts
COTTAGE CHEESE, LARGE CURD, drained	3 quarts
BLEU CHEESE, crumbled	12 ounces
WATERCRESS, chopped	3 cups
PARSLEY, chopped	3 cups

Procedure

1. Crumble ripe olives coarsely with fingers.

2. Mix with remaining ingredients. Chill several hours. (Mixture may be scooped or spread in a pan and cut into squares.)

For Ripe Olive Tomato Salad with Shrimp:

1. Arrange large tomato half on plate in center of 5 romaine leaves arranged spoke-fashion.

2. Arrange shrimp, ripe olives, sliced cucumber, marinated cooked diced carrots and hot chili peppers on separate leaves.

3. Top tomato with a No. 8 or No. 10 scoop Ripe Olive Cheese Salad.

For Ripe Olive Pineapple Salad with Shrimp:

1. Place 2 drained canned pineapple slices in center of lettuce lined plate.

2. Top with a No. 8 or No. 10 scoop of Ripe Olive Cheese Salad.

3. Arrange shrimp around pineapple.

4. Garnish with radish, hot chili pepper, sweet gherkin and ripe olive.

For Ripe Olive Cucumber Salad with Shrimp:

1. Arrange shrimp, sliced cucumbers and marinated cooked diced carrots on crisp salad greens as desired.

2. Place a rectangular cut of Ripe Olive Cheese Salad in center.

3. Garnish with whole ripe olives.

VEGETABLE SALADS

VARIETY in eye-teasing, taste-pleasing salads comes easily when vegetables—raw and/or cooked—highlight the ingredient list.

Among the raw vegetables, tomato and cucumber salads and the cabbage slaws have a loyal following. But don't overlook the possibilities with cauliflower, spinach leaves and shredded carrots.

An amazing number of bright, flavorsome vegetables, cooked just to the crisp-tender stage, lend themselves to imaginative salad making. Many await in cans, ready to chill and use. Feature them in arranged salads or tossed salad mixtures. Team them with cool, crisp raw vegetables or other salad materials such as scoops of cottage cheese or slices of hard-cooked egg.

Much of the success of cooked vegetable salads stems from their color, flavor and texture. Top quality vegetables in neat, evenly-cut pieces and fresh, perky greens are absolute "musts." Marinating cooked vegetables briefly in a well seasoned oil and vinegar dressing zips up the flavor and brightens the looks.

You can create colorful, savory salad mixtures by com-

bining two or more vegetables and adding celery, cucumber or other crisp foods to give a desirable "crunch." Toss lightly with a clear, sparkly dressing or with mayonnaise perked with sour cream. Use salads of this nature to fill individual tomato aspic rings or to stuff fresh tomatoes. Feature them as entree salads, or as accompaniments to cold seafood, poultry or meats. And take advantage of their interesting potential for the cold buffet.

MARINATED VEGETABLE SALAD

Yield: 48 portions

Ingredients

CARROTS, whole, peeled	4 pounds
POLE BEANS, whole, trimmed	3 pounds
WHITE TURNIPS, peeled	1 pound
PEAS, FRESH, shelled	1¾ quarts
CELERY, diced	3 cups
ONIONS, finely chopped	2 cups
SALAD OIL	2 cups
TARRAGON VINEGAR	1 cup
WATER	½ cup
PARSLEY, chopped	¼ cup
LEMON JUICE	2 tablespoons
SALT	1 tablespoon
BLACK PEPPER, ground	½ teaspoon

Procedure

1. Cook whole carrots, whole pole beans, whole turnips and peas separately, until crisp-tender. Do not overcook. Cool quickly.

2. Dice carrots, beans and turnips. Combine with peas, celery and onions.

3. Combine salad oil, vinegar, water, parsley, lemon juice, salt and pepper; mix well. Pour over vegetables; stir gently.

4. Refrigerate 4 to 6 hours.

RED KIDNEY BEAN SALAD

Yield: 25 portions

Ingredients

RED KIDNEY BEANS, washed and drained	1 No. 10 can
SALT	2 teaspoons
CELERY, sliced, cut medium	2 cups
SWEET RELISH	1 cup
EGGS, hard-cooked, cut medium	8
MAYONNAISE	about 2 cups
EGG SLICES	25

Procedure

1. Combine first five ingredients. Add mayonnaise and toss lightly.
2. Serve on leaf lettuce. Top with egg slices.

RAW SPINACH SALAD

Yield: 20 1/3-cup portions

Ingredients

CELERY, chopped fine	1 cup
ONIONS, chopped fine	1 cup
EGGS, hard-cooked, chopped	6
AMERICAN CHEESE, processed, sharp, cubed small	1½ cups
SPINACH, chopped fine	2 quarts
SALT	1 teaspoon
HOT PEPPER SAUCE	1 teaspoon
VINEGAR, WHITE	1 tablespoon
MAYONNAISE	2½ to 3 cups
PREPARED HORSERADISH	½ cup
EGGS, hard-cooked, grated	6

Procedure

1. Combine celery, onions, eggs and cheese. Mix with spinach.
2. Combine salt, hot pepper sauce, vinegar and mayonnaise. Mix well. Add to first mixture and fold lightly. Serve on lettuce leaf.
3. Garnish with teaspoon of horseradish on side. Add 1 tablespoon grated egg on top of each salad.

RAW VEGETABLE SALAD

Yield: 32 portions

Ingredients

LETTUCE	2¼ pounds
SPINACH	14 ounces
ROMAINE	10 ounces
CELERY, crescents	1¼ pounds
TOMATOES, cut in wedges	2¼ pounds
WATERCRESS	3 ounces
LEMON JUICE	¼ cup
SALT	2 teaspoons
WHITE PEPPER	¼ teaspoon
DRY MUSTARD	1 teaspoon
MAYONNAISE	2 cups

Procedure

1. Cut lettuce, spinach, and romaine into bite-size pieces.
2. Add other vegetables.
3. Mix seasonings with mayonnaise. Add to salad greens just before serving.

PICKLED BEETS

Yield: about 3 quarts

Ingredients

BEETS, sliced	1 No. 10 can
SUGAR	3 cups
VINEGAR	3 cups
SALT	2 tablespoons
PEPPER	1/8 teaspoon
ONION JUICE	1 teaspoon

Procedure

1. Drain beets. Add sugar, vinegar, salt, pepper and onion juice (from grated onion) to liquid drained from beets. Stir to dissolve sugar and salt.
2. Pour seasoned liquid over sliced beets. Allow to stand in refrigerator 24 hours before using.

ITALIAN SALAD

Yield: 24 portions

Ingredients

GREEN BEANS, cut, cooked	1 quart
CARROTS, cooked, diced	1 quart
CELERY, chopped	1 quart
PEAS, cooked	2 cups
CUCUMBERS, peeled, diced	2 cups
MAYONNAISE	1 cup
SOUR CREAM	½ cup

Procedure

1. Combine vegetables.

2. Blend mayonnaise and sour cream. Pour over vegetables; toss together lightly. Chill well to blend flavors.

3. Serve in lettuce cups.

CINNAMON TOMATO SALAD

Yield: 48 portions

Ingredients

TOMATOES, medium	48
SALT	3 tablespoons
BLACK PEPPER, ground	2 teaspoons
SUGAR	2 cups
CINNAMON, ground	2 tablespoons
VINEGAR	2 cups
SALAD OIL	½ cup
CRISP SALAD GREENS	as needed
PARSLEY FLAKES	1 cup

Procedure

1. Slice tomatoes thin. Sprinkle with salt and pepper. Let stand for 10 minutes; drain.

2. Mix sugar and cinnamon. Add vinegar and oil; mix until well blended. Pour over tomatoes. Marinate in refrigerator for 1 hour or longer. Drain.

3. Serve on crisp greens. Sprinkle with parsley.

NORTH BEACH PINEAPPLE 'N BEAN SALAD

Yield: 48 portions

Ingredients

PINEAPPLE CHUNKS	1 No. 10 can
RED KIDNEY BEANS	4 1-pound cans
LIMA BEANS, FROZEN	2½ pounds
GREEN BEANS, CUT, FROZEN	2½ pounds
GREEN PEPPERS, cut in chunks	4
CELERY, sliced	1 quart
CORNSTARCH	¼ cup
MUSTARD, DRY	¼ cup
PEPPER	2 teaspoons
DILL WEED	2 teaspoons
SUGAR	3 tablespoons
SEASONED SALT	4 teaspoons
WINE VINEGAR	1 cup
SYRUP FROM PINEAPPLE	2 cups
OLIVE OIL	1 cup

Procedure

1. Drain pineapple, reserving required amount of syrup.
2. Drain kidney beans.
3. Cook lima beans and cut green beans until just tender; *do not overcook.* Drain.
4. Combine pineapple and vegetables. Cover. Chill.
5. Mix cornstarch and seasonings; blend with vinegar; add pineapple syrup. Cook and stir over moderate heat until thickened.
6. Remove from heat; beat in olive oil. Chill.
7. When ready to serve, toss vegetable mixture with dressing.

SNAPPY BEAN SALAD ⟶

Yield: 32 ½-cup portions

Ingredients

WAX BEANS, diagonal cut, drained	1 No. 10 can
OLIVES, RIPE, chopped	1 cup
CELERY, diced	1 cup
ITALIAN-STYLE SALAD DRESSING, bottled	1 cup

FLAMINGO SALAD

Yield: 25 ¾-cup portions

Ingredients

CUCUMBERS	3 pounds
ONIONS, SWEET	½ pound
GREEN PEPPERS	1½ pounds
TOMATOES	3 pounds

Procedure

1. Peel cucumbers; score and cut in very thin slices.
2. Cut onions in very thin slices; separate into rings.
3. Cut green peppers in half; remove core, seeds and white membrane. Slice in very thin strips.
4. Cut each tomato in wedges.
5. Toss all vegetables together in large salad bowl with 2 large wooden forks to avoid crushing vegetables.
6. Serve in individual salad bowls with Sour Cream Dressing.*

*SOUR CREAM DRESSING

Yield: 2 cups

Ingredients

SOUR CREAM	1 pint
SALT	2 teaspoons
SUGAR	1½ teaspoons
PEPPER	¼ teaspoon
PAPRIKA	½ teaspoon
DRY MUSTARD	½ teaspoon
WORCESTERSHIRE SAUCE	1½ teaspoons
HOT PEPPER SAUCE	few drops

Procedure

1. Combine sour cream and seasonings, mixing well.

Procedure

1. Combine wax beans, olives and celery in a shallow pan.
2. Drizzle with salad dressing. Refrigerate thoroughly or overnight.
3. Stir gently before serving in lettuce cups or on crisp salad greens.

VINEGAR RELISH SALAD

Yield: 5 gallons, 107 6-ounce portions

Ingredients

VINEGAR	2¾ quarts
ICE WATER	2¾ quarts
SUGAR	12 ounces
SALT	3 ounces
PEPPER	1 tablespoon
CUCUMBERS, peeled	14 pounds
ONIONS, peeled	5 pounds
RADISHES	1½ pounds
GREEN PEPPERS, trimmed, seeded	1½ pounds
CARROTS, peeled	5 pounds
CAULIFLOWER	3 pounds

Procedure

1. Combine vinegar, water, sugar, salt and pepper.
2. Slice cucumbers, onions, radishes, green peppers and carrots as thinly as possible (less than 1/8-inch). Break cauliflower into very small flowerettes.
3. Alternate raw vegetables in layers; pour on vinegar mixture. Chill thoroughly for at least 1 hour. Toss lightly before transferring to large (10-inch) salad bowls or other containers for service.

Garnish

Sprinkle chopped parsley over top. Stir lightly to mix parsley with top layer. Sprinkle well-drained julienne strips of pickled beets over top.

SPICED BEET AND AVOCADO SALAD

Yield: 100 portions

Ingredients

SPICED BEETS	2 No. 10 cans
LEAF LETTUCE	5 to 6 heads
AVOCADOS, No. 16 COUNT	12

Procedure

1. Arrange 4 or 5 slices of spiced beets on leaf lettuce.
2. Cut 2 slices of avocado and place over the sliced beets.
3. Serve with 1 ounce souffle cup of French dressing.

GREEN PEA SALAD

Yield: 20 portions

Ingredients

SALT	1 teaspoon
GARLIC	1 clove
PEPPER, WHITE	1 teaspoon
ONIONS, finely chopped	½ cup
SOUR CREAM	2 cups or more
GREEN PEAS, FROZEN, cooked	1¾ quarts
ONION RINGS, small	60
PARSLEY SPRIGS	20

Procedure

1. Put salt in salad bowl. Crush garlic into salt.
2. Add pepper and onion and sour cream. Mix well.
3. Add to peas and toss lightly.
4. Serve on lettuce leaf. Garnish top of each salad with 3 small onion rings and parsley on side.

VEGETABLE PATCH SALAD

Yield: 50 portions

Ingredients

BRUSSELS SPROUTS, FROZEN	8 pounds
CORN, WHOLE KERNEL	1½ No. 10 cans
ONIONS, chopped	1 pound
CUCUMBERS, peeled, seeded, chopped	1 pound
GREEN PEPPERS, chopped	8 ounces
PIMIENTOES, chopped	1 cup
FRENCH DRESSING	1 quart
CRISP SALAD GREENS	as needed

Procedure

1. Cook Brussels sprouts until just tender. Drain. Cool; cut in halves.
2. Drain corn. Combine with Brussels sprouts, onion, cucumber, green pepper, pimiento and French dressing. Chill thoroughly.
3. Serve on salad greens.

Note

If desired, add 5 pounds diced chicken, turkey or tuna.

SALAD DU GRAND GEANE

Yield: 6 quarts

Ingredients

GREEN BEANS, sliced, drained	1 No. 10 can
CORN, WHOLE KERNEL, drained	1/2 No. 10 can
PEAS, drained	1/2 No. 10 can
ONIONS, SPANISH, sliced	3 large
CELERY, diced	2 cups
SALT	2-2/3 tablespoons
SUGAR	1 cup
VINEGAR, WINE	1 cup
SALAD OIL	2-1/2 cups

Procedure

1. Combine drained canned vegetables with onions and celery; toss lightly to mix. Spread mixture evenly in shallow pans.

2. Combine salt, sugar and vinegar; stir to dissolve. Add salad oil; mix well.

3. Pour dressing over vegetables. Chill 4 to 5 hours, stirring occasionally. Serve in lettuce cups.

BACON 'N VEGETABLE SALAD

Yield: 24 portions

Ingredients

BACON, sliced	3 pounds
LETTUCE, torn in pieces	1¾ gallons
MIXED VEGETABLES, cooked, chilled	2¼ pounds
CELERY, sliced	1 quart
GREEN ONIONS, sliced	½ cup
OIL and VINEGAR DRESSING	1½ cups
EGGS, hard-cooked, sliced	12

Procedure

1. Cook bacon until crisp; crumble coarsely.

2. Combine lettuce, mixed vegetables, celery and green onions. Toss lightly with oil and vinegar dressing.

3. Add bacon and sliced eggs. Toss lightly until mixed. Serve at once.

CUCUMBER SOUR CREAM SALAD

Yield: 24 portions

Ingredients

CUCUMBERS	10 medium
SALT	1/4 cup
VINEGAR, CIDER	1/3 cup
SUGAR	2-1/2 teaspoons
BLACK PEPPER, ground	3/4 teaspoon
INSTANT GARLIC POWDER	1/4 teaspoon
SOUR CREAM	3-3/4 cups

Procedure

1. Cut unpeeled cucumbers in slices 1/8-inch thick. Sprinkle with salt and vinegar. Let stand 3 hours. Drain.

2. Combine sugar, black pepper, garlic powder and sour cream. Add to cucumbers; toss lightly to blend.

3 BEAN SALAD

Yield: 50 ½-cup portions

Ingredients

GREEN BEANS, diagonal cut, drained	2½ quarts
WAX BEANS, diagonal cut, drained	2½ quarts
KIDNEY BEANS, drained	1 quart
ONIONS, sliced	1 cup
GREEN PEPPERS, chopped	1 cup
PIMIENTOES, chopped	½ cup
WINE VINEGAR	1½ cups
SALAD OIL	1½ cups
SUGAR	1 cup
SALT	2 tablespoons

Procedure

1. Combine beans, onions, green peppers and pimientoes; toss together lightly.

2. Combine vinegar, oil, sugar and salt. Shake or beat until sugar and salt are dissolved.

3. Pour dressing over bean mixture; toss until vegetables are coated. Marinate, refrigerated, 4 hours or overnight.

RAW CAULIFLOWER SALAD

Yield: 20 1/3-cup portions

Ingredients

CAULIFLOWER, flowerettes	1½ quarts
CELERY, sliced	3 cups
TOKAY GRAPES, halved and seeded	3 cups
SALT	1 teaspoon
MAYONNAISE	2½ cups

Procedure

1. Break or cut cauliflower into bite-size flowerettes, add celery, grapes and salt. Mix well.

2. Add mayonnaise and toss. Serve on leaf lettuce.

SWEET SOUR GREEN BEAN SALAD

Yield: 15 ¾-cup portions

Ingredients

GREEN BEANS, BLUE LAKE, french style or cut	1 No. 10 can
VINEGAR, CIDER	1 quart
LIQUOR FROM CANNED BEANS	1 cup
SUGAR, GRANULATED	1 pound, 14 ounces
SALT	1 tablespoon
ONIONS, WHITE, thinly sliced	8 ounces
SALT	1 tablespoon
SALAD OIL	½ cup
SPECIAL DRESSING	2 cups

Procedure

1. Drain green beans reserving required amount of liquor.

2. To prepare special dressing, heat vinegar and bean liquor; add sugar and first amount of salt. Stir until sugar dissolves. Chill thoroughly.*

3. Combine drained green beans and onions.

4. Add remaining salt, salad oil and special dressing. Toss lightly to mix.

5. Refrigerate at least 30 minutes. Serve as a salad in lettuce cup, if desired. Or serve in a side dish as salad or relish.

*This special dressing can be made in quantity and kept on hand for use.

GREEN BEANS VINAIGRETTE

Yield: 24 portions

Ingredients

GREEN BEANS, BLUE LAKE, whole or French style	1 No. 10 can
SALAD OIL	1½ cups
VINEGAR	1 cup
SALT	2 teaspoons
SUGAR	1 tablespoon
SWEET PICKLE RELISH	1/3 cup
PIMIENTOES, chopped	1/4 cup

Procedure

1. Drain green beans.

2. Beat oil, vinegar, salt and sugar together; add pickle relish and pimiento.

3. Combine dressing and drained green beans; let stand for several hours. Serve cold. (Use salad greens or not, as desired).

GARBANZO BEAN SALAD

Yield: 3 gallons

Ingredients

GARBANZOS	1 No. 10 can
GREEN BEANS, cut	1 No. 10 can
YELLOW WAX BEANS, cut	1 No. 10 can
ONIONS, thinly sliced	3 cups
GREEN BELL PEPPERS, chopped	3 cups
SALAD OIL	2 cups
VINEGAR	1 quart
SUGAR	4½ cups
SALT	2 tablespoons
PEPPER, BLACK	1 tablespoon

Procedure

1. Wash and drain garbanzos. Drain green and wax beans.

2. Combine garbanzos, beans, onions and green peppers.

3. Combine oil, vinegar, sugar, salt and pepper. Add to vegetable mixture; toss to mix thoroughly.

4. Cover; refrigerate overnight.

5. Drain before serving.

GREEN BEAN SALAD

Yield: 12 portions

Ingredients

ONION, minced	2 tablespoons
VINEGAR and OIL DRESSING	½ cup
MAYONNAISE	½ cup
GREEN BEANS, cooked	2 quarts
EGGS, hard-cooked, coarsely chopped	4
SALT	as needed
PEPPER	as needed

Procedure

1. Combine onion, oil dressing and mayonnaise. Pour over green beans; marinate 1 hour.

2. Add eggs; toss together to mix. Season to taste with salt and pepper.

GREEN BEANS MANDARIN

Yield: 24 portions

Ingredients

GREEN BEANS, BLUE LAKE, cut	1 No. 10 can
MANDARIN ORANGE SEGMENTS	4 11-ounce cans
LIQUID FROM CANNED BEANS	1 cup
SYRUP FROM MANDARIN ORANGES	½ cup
WINE VINEGAR	½ cup
SALAD OIL	1 cup
ONION, raw, finely chopped	½ cup
or INSTANT MINCED ONION	2 tablespoons
SALT	1½ teaspoons
LETTUCE, shredded	1½ pounds

Procedure

1. Drain green beans and orange segments, reserving required amount of liquids.

2. Combine liquid from beans, orange syrup, wine vinegar, salad oil, onion and salt. Pour over green beans and orange sections. Marinate in refrigerator several hours or overnight.

3. Drain. Serve green beans and orange mixture on shredded lettuce. Use drained marinade as dressing.

PETER PAN SALAD

Yield: 48 2/3-cup portions

Ingredients

PEAS, frozen*	5 pounds
SALAD DRESSING	3 cups
DILL PICKLES (KOSHER), chopped	3 cups
INSTANT CHOPPED ONION	½ cup
SALT	1 tablespoon
EGGS, hard-cooked, coarsely chopped	32
CHEESE, AMERICAN, diced	2 pounds
RADISHES, thinly sliced	10 ounces

Procedure

1. Cook peas, drain. Chill.
2. Combine salad dressing, pickles, instant onion and salt; blend.
3. Combine peas, eggs, cheese and radishes. Add salad dressing mixture; mix gently. Chill.
4. Serve on crisp salad greens. Garnish with hard-cooked egg slices, radish roses or ripe olives, if desired.

*Or 2 No. 10 cans peas, drained.

MARINATED CUCUMBERS

Yield: 32 1/3-cup portions

Ingredients

SALAD OIL	¾ cup
VINEGAR	3 cups
SUGAR	3 cups
SALT	2 teaspoons
WHITE PEPPER	2 teaspoons
CUCUMBERS, unpeeled, scored with fork and sliced	3 quarts
ONIONS, cut in half lengthwise and sliced	2½ cups

Procedure

1. Make a dressing of oil, vinegar, sugar, salt and pepper. Pour over the cucumbers and onions and toss lightly. Marinate 2 to 3 hours.
2. Serve on shredded lettuce on plate lined with leaf lettuce.

Tomato Petals Frame Crab Salad

Alaska King Crab Marketing and Quality Control Board

Stuffed Tomato Salads

A LARGE, well-shaped, ripe tomato transforms a modest amount of hearty salad into a full-fledged cold entree. Little wonder that stuffed tomatoes are a favorite for luncheon salad meals!

There are many ways to prepare a tomato that is to be stuffed: Peel it or leave the skin on. Cut it in layer-cake, fan-tan, cup or petal fashion. Vary the filling—there are so many taste-tempting combinations attractive to serve.

Serving unpeeled tomatoes cuts preparation time to a minimum. But a peeled tomato has a high t-l-c quotient, and peeling tomatoes is far from a chore. Merely place tomatoes in a wire basket and lower them into boiling water. (A steam jacketed kettle is ideal for this; the water comes back to boiling with hardly a pause.) Hold the tomatoes immersed in the boiling water while counting slowly to seven. (Put an "and" between the numbers as, one-and-two-and-three, etc.) Lift the basket out and rub a thumb over a tomato to test for loosened skin. Return to the boiling water, if necessary, but be careful not to overdo it. As soon as the tomatoes are scalded, i.e. the skins respond properly to the thumb test, plunge tomatoes into cold water at once. Chill until needed.

Peel tomatoes just before using. The flavor begins to deteriorate once the flesh is exposed to air. Another reason for not peeling ahead: if scalded but unpeeled tomatoes are not used, they keep in good condition until the next day.

Layer-cake and fan-tan designs make attractive stuffed tomatoes for specialty use, but they require a little care to cut and fill. Closely-knit fillings like chopped egg salad and creamed cottage cheese work out best for these styles. To make the layer-cake type, first cut the tomato crosswise into three slices. Place the filling between the slices stacking them layer cake fashion. For the fan-tan, slice the tomato into ½-in. vertical slices, almost through to the bottom. Spread out the slices; place the filling between them.

Tomatoes hollowed out to make a cup, or cut down and opened out in petal design, lend themselves to any number of fillings easily portioned with a scoop. Petal-cut stuffed tomatoes look larger, are easier to eat and have the nice faculty of staying balanced on the plate. (See picture, p. 128.)

To make a cup, cut a slice off the stem end of the tomato and scoop out the pulp with a small spoon, leaving a cup. Or, cut around the top and deep into the tomato, keeping the knife slanted towards the center to cut a cone-shaped piece which lifts out to form a cup. To make a petal shape, simply remove core from tomato. Cut in six sections almost to the bottom. Spread sections apart and fill.

As for fillings, here are a few suggestions:
Ham salad with capers
Turkey salad topped with chopped roasted almonds
Savory egg salad
Mixed cooked vegetables tossed with mayonnaise
Potato salad topped with crisp bacon bits
*Cottage cheese mixed with deviled ham or finely
    cut raw vegetables*
Curried shrimp salad
Chicken vegetable salad
Green pepper cole slaw
Marinated King crab and celery

BACON-CHEESE STUFFED TOMATOES

Yield: 18 portions (No. 16 scoop)

Ingredients

BACON, sliced	1 pound
COTTAGE CHEESE	1½ pounds
AVOCADOS, cut in cubes	2
TOMATOES, whole	18

Procedure

1. Cut bacon into 1-inch pieces. Pan fry until crisp. Drain on absorbent paper.

3. Combine bacon pieces, cottage cheese and avocado.

3. Cut tomatoes into wedges from stem end almost to bottom. Set each tomato on a lettuce-lined salad plate. Separate wedges slightly; fill centers with a No. 16 scoop of cheese mixture.

Note

Use filling to fill aspic rings or serve on sliced tomatoes, if desired.

TOMATO MIXED VEGETABLE SALAD

Yield: 48 portions

Ingredients

CARROTS, cooked, diced	2 pounds
POTATOES, cooked, diced	2 pounds
POLE BEANS, cooked, diced	2 pounds
CELERY, diced	8 ounces
FRENCH DRESSING	1 quart
TOMATOES, medium	48
LETTUCE	as needed

Procedure

1. Combine carrots, potatoes, pole beans and celery; add dressing. Toss lightly to mix.

2. Refrigerate 2 hours, stirring frequently. Drain.

3. Core tomatoes. Cut into 6 sections almost to, but not through, the bottom. Spread apart slightly.

4. Place tomatoes on lettuce-lined plates. Fill with marinated vegetables. Garnish with mayonnaise, if desired.

Potato Salads

POTATO salads are a ready answer for a main-dish attraction on warm-to-torrid summer days. New versions of this perennial favorite give it new interest as a menu listing. And for easier, quicker preparation, potatoes in modern form are an added advantage. Processed potatoes—peeled and cut, needing only reconstituting—shorten preparation time and help relieve the peak-season salad room rush.

A well-seasoned potato salad, with a pleasing arrangement of cold meats, is a welcome addition to warm weather luncheon or supper menus. With today's varied selection of ready-to-eat meats and almost bewildering variety of cheeses, cold plates need never lack interest if the salad has a just-made freshness, is displayed on cool crisp greens and carries a colorful garnish.

For a different approach, make a meat and potato salad (the meat in the salad) and serve it in a salad bowl. Ham, tuna or crabmeat tossed with potato salad makes an appetite-teasing meal-in-one dish.

And, for another change, make a hot potato salad and feature it with frankfurters, mettwurst or similar meats.

SHRIMP-POTATO SALAD (with eggs and cheese)

Yield: approximately 4 gallons

Ingredients

SHRIMP, cooked, cleaned	5½ pounds (4½ quarts)
POTATOES, cooked, diced	2¼ gallons
EGGS, hard-cooked, chopped	48
CELERY, chopped	3½ pounds (3½ quarts)
ONIONS, chopped	12 ounces (2 cups)
SWEET PICKLE RELISH, undrained	1¾ cups
CHEESE, grated	1 pound
MAYONNAISE or SALAD DRESSING	1¾ quarts
SALT	as needed

Procedure

1. Cut shrimp into ½-inch pieces.
2. Combine all ingredients; salt to taste.
3. Chill for at least 1 hour to allow potatoes to absorb dressing.
4. Serve No. 30 scoop on antipasto plates or in center of individual tomato aspic rings. Or, serve No. 8 or No. 6 scoop as main dish salad.

SHRIMP POTATO SALAD

Yield: 2 gallons (50 2/3-cup portions)

Ingredients

DEHYDRATED SLICED POTATOES	1 2¼-pound package
SALAD OIL	1½ cups
VINEGAR	1 cup
SHRIMP, cooked	3 pounds
CELERY, diced	1 quart
ONIONS, chopped	1 cup
DILL PICKLE, chopped	1 cup
HOT PEPPER SAUCE	1 teaspoon
WHITE PEPPER	1 teaspoon
MAYONNAISE	1 quart

Procedure

1. Cook potatoes according to package directions; drain. Add salad oil and vinegar; mix lightly. Cool.
2. Add remaining ingredients; mix well. Chill thoroughly.

KING CRAB POTATO SALAD

Yield: 48 portions

Ingredients

VINEGAR	1 cup
MAYONNAISE	1 cup
SUGAR	¼ cup
MUSTARD, DRY	2 teaspoons
PAPRIKA	1 tablespoon
PEPPER	2 teaspoons
SALT	2 tablespoons
CHIVES, chopped	2 tablespoons
SALAD OIL	3 cups
KING CRAB MEAT	3 quarts
POTATOES, DEHYDRATED SLICES, cooked according to package directions	1½ gallons
ITALIAN GREEN BEANS, FROZEN, cut, cooked	1½ quarts
CELERY, sliced	1 quart
OLIVES, STUFFED, sliced	2 cups

Procedure

1. Combine vinegar, mayonnaise, seasonings and chives. Add oil; blend until smooth.

2. Combine crab meat, potatoes, green beans, celery and olives. Pour dressing over mixture; toss to mix. Chill.

3. Serve on crisp salad greens. Garnish with hard-cooked egg, tomato wedges and slices of crab leg, as desired.

EASY POTATO SALAD ⟶

Yield: 1½ gallons

Ingredients

SLICED INSTANT POTATOES	1 2¼ pound package
VINEGAR	1 cup
CELERY, diced	1 quart
ONIONS, chopped	½ cup
PEPPER, WHITE	1 teaspoon
LIQUID HOT PEPPER SEASONING	1 teaspoon
MAYONNAISE	1 quart

MEAT 'N POTATO SALAD

Yield: approximately 12 quarts

Ingredients

THURINGER or COOKED SALAMI SAUSAGE, thinly sliced	2¼ pounds
FRENCH DRESSING	1½ cups
POTATOES, cooked, sliced or cut in cubes	12 pounds (2¼ gallons)
ONIONS, chopped	¾ cup
CELERY, chopped	1 quart
PIMIENTO OLIVES, sliced	48 (1¾ cups)
SWEET PICKLES, chopped	3 cups
EGGS, hard-cooked sliced	20
SALT	¼ cup
SALAD DRESSING	1¼ quarts
SWEET PICKLE JUICE	½ cup
PREPARED MUSTARD	¼ cup

Procedure

1. Cut thuringer or salami into small pieces.

2. Pour French dressing over potatoes; toss to coat each piece thoroughly. Let stand 2 hours in refrigerator.

3. Add meat, onion, celery, olives, pickles, eggs and salt. Mix well.

4. Combine salad dressing, pickle juice and mustard. Pour over potato mixture. Mix lightly and thoroughly. Chill.

Procedure

1. Cook potatoes according to package directions. Drain well. Add vinegar; mix lightly. Cool.

2. Add celery to the potatoes.

3. Mix onions, seasonings and mayonnaise. Pour over vegetables; mix well. Chill.

Note

To vary, add sliced stuffed olives, diced cucumbers or hard-cooked eggs, or chopped parsley, pimientoes or green peppers.

METTWURST AND HOT POTATO SALAD

Yield: 32 portions

Ingredients

POTATOES, peeled	7½ pounds
BACON, diced	6 ounces
ONIONS, chopped	4 ounces
MARGARINE	3 ounces
FLOUR	3 ounces
HOT WATER	3 cups
VINEGAR	1¼ cups
SUGAR	2¼ ounces
SALT	4 teaspoons
WHITE PEPPER	¾ teaspoons
GREEN ONIONS, sliced thin	5 ounces
PARSLEY, chopped	1¼ ounces
METTWURST	

Procedure

1. Steam potatoes; dice while hot.

2. Fry bacon until crisp and remove from fat. Add onions; saute until done. Add margarine and flour, cook slowly.

3. Add water, stir until thick.

4. Add vinegar and seasonings, mix thoroughly.

5. Pour sauce over potatoes and keep hot.

6. Put potatoes in steam table pan, top with bacon, parsley, and onion. Serve with mettwurst links.

Potato Salads Make Good Filling for Tomatoes

General Foods Corp.

VEGETABLE POTATO SALAD

Yield: 60 2/3-cup portions

Ingredients

DEHYDRATED SLICED POTATOES	2-1/4 pounds
FROZEN GREEN PEAS, cooked	2 quarts
CARROTS, cooked, diced	2 quarts
CELERY, diced	2 quarts
PARSLEY, chopped	1 quart (12 ounces)
MAYONNAISE	1-1/4 quarts
ONION, grated	1/3 cup
LEMON JUICE	1/3 cup
SALT	2-1/2 tablespoons
PEPPER	1-1/2 teaspoons
SOUR CREAM	1 quart

Procedure

1. Cook potatoes according to package directions; drain well. Cool.
2. Add peas, carrots, celery and parsley.
3. Mix mayonnaise, seasonings and sour cream. Pour over vegetables; toss lightly. Chill.
4. Serve on crisp salad greens. Top with a slice of hard-cooked egg and a sprinkling of chopped parsley, if desired.

HOT POTATO-PIMIENTO SALAD

Yield: 50 portions

Ingredients

POTATOES, raw, unpeeled	12 pounds
BACON, chopped	1 pound
CELERY, diced	1 pound
ONIONS, finely chopped	8 ounces
FLOUR	1 cup
VINEGAR, CIDER	1 cup
BEEF STOCK, hot	2 cups
SEASONED PEPPER	1/2 teaspoon
SALT	as needed
CAYENNE	1/8 teaspoon
PIMIENTOES, diced	1 quart
PARSLEY, chopped	1/2 cup
PAPRIKA	as needed

Procedure

1. Cook unpeeled potatoes. Cool slightly. Remove skins; slice while still hot.

2. Fry bacon slowly until crisp. Drain off about half the fat from pan. Immediately add bacon and remaining fat to hot potatoes.

3. Add celery and onion; mix lightly but well.

4. Blend flour and vinegar; stir into hot stock. Cook and stir until thickened and smooth.

5. Add seasonings, continue to cook for another minute. Pour hot dressing over potatoes. Add pimiento; fold gently to mix.

6. Turn into steam table pans. Sprinkle with parsley, then with paprika.

FRANKS AND HOT POTATO SALAD

Yield: 50 portions

Ingredients

POTATOES, cubed	11½ pounds
SALT	¼ cup
GREEN PEPPERS, diced	1½ cups
PIMIENTOES, diced	¾ cup
EGGS, hard-cooked, diced	12
BACON, sliced	10 ounces
ONIONS, diced	1½ cups
FLOUR	½ cup
VINEGAR, CIDER	2¼ cups
WATER	2¼ cups
SUGAR	1½ cups
SALT	2 tablespoons
CELERY SEED	1½ teaspoons
FRANKS, 8's	12 pounds

Procedure

1. Cook potatoes in water to which the ¼-cup salt has been added. Drain.

2. Combine potatoes, green pepper, pimiento and hard-cooked eggs; keep hot.

3. Cut bacon slices into ½-inch pieces and cook until almost crisp. Add onion and cook until clear. Remove bacon and onion from drippings.

4. Blend the flour into the bacon drippings. Remove from heat. Add vinegar, water, sugar, the 2 tablespoons of salt and celery seed. Mix well; return to heat and cook until flour taste has disappeared. Add the bacon and onion.

5. Pour hot sauce over hot potatoes; mix carefully.

6. Heat franks, but do not boil.

7. Allow 2 franks per portion, with 2/3 cup of hot salad.

TUNA POTATO SALAD

Yield: 2 gallons, 50 2/3-cup portions

Ingredients

DEHYDRATED SLICED POTATOES	1 package (2¼ pounds)
SALT	¼ cup
WATER	2 gallons
SALAD OIL	1½ cups
VINEGAR	1 cup
TUNA FISH, drained, flaked	3 pounds 6 ounces (2½ quarts)
CELERY, diced	1 quart
ONIONS, chopped	1 cup
DILL PICKLE, chopped	1 cup
SALT (OPTIONAL)	1 to 1½ tablespoons
HOT PEPPER SAUCE	1 teaspoon
PEPPER, WHITE	1 teaspoon
MAYONNAISE	1 quart

Procedure

1. Cook potatoes with salt and water as directed on package. Drain well. Add oil and vinegar; mix lightly. Cool.

2. Add remaining ingredients; mix thoroughly. Chill.

3. Serve on crisp greens. Garnish with parsley, tomato wedges or radish roses, as desired.

HAM POTATO SALAD

Yield: 2 gallons, 50 2/3-cup portions

Ingredients

DEHYDRATED SLICED POTATOES	1 package (2¼ pounds)
SALT	¼ cup
WATER	2 gallons
SALAD OIL	1½ cups
VINEGAR	1 cup
HAM, cooked, diced	2 pounds
GREEN PEPPERS, chopped	1 cup
CELERY, diced	1 quart
ONIONS, chopped	1 cup
SALT	1 to 1½ tablespoons
PEPPER, WHITE	1 teaspoon
HOT PEPPER SAUCE	1 teaspoon
MAYONNAISE	1 quart

Procedure

1. Cook potatoes with salt and water as directed on the package. Drain well. Add oil and vinegar; mix lightly. Cool.

2. Add remaining ingredients; mix lightly but thoroughly. Chill.

3. Serve on crisp greens. Garnish with parsley, tomato wedges or radish roses, as desired.

Variation

For Ham and Cheese Potato Salad use above recipe decreasing ham to 1¼ pounds (1 quart) and adding ½ pound (2 cups) cubed cheddar cheese.

Slaw as Side Dish

American Spice Trade Assn.

Slaw as Main Dish

Campbell Soup Co.

Slaws

CRISP, savory slaws begin with firm textured cabbage. A prime head is tightly packed, making the head solid and fairly heavy for its size. It is also well trimmed, with the stem cut close to the head and all but three or four of the wrapping leaves removed.

Before shredding, halve or quarter the heads and cut out the core by making a "V" cut with the tip of the knife. Machine equipment can easily slice through the core, but a far better slaw results when the hard core portion of the cabbage is removed.

White, green and red cabbages all make attractive slaws. Cabbage that's cut and marketed immediately has green leaves; stored, mature cabbage is white. During the winter months all three types are available. This gives the opportunity to increase variety and introduce color by simply changing the cabbage or by mixing two types. (See chart, next page, for this and other variations of basic slaw.)

For best texture and appearance make cole slaw up fresh for each meal. Do not attempt to hold it over for the second day. And, for best flavor, allow slaw to marinate in its dressing at least an hour before serving. Turn it occasionally. Keep cut cabbage or slaw tightly covered while in refrigerator to prevent giving the stronger odors of cabbage to other foods.

BASIC COLE SLAW

Yield: 1 gallon, 32 ½-cup portions

Ingredients

		Procedure
CABBAGE, shredded	7 pounds (7 quarts)	1. Crisp cabbage in ice water. Drain thoroughly.
MAYONNAISE	¾ quart	2. Combine mayonnaise, lemon juice and seasonings. Pour over cabbage; toss to mix.
LEMON JUICE, fresh	1/3 cup	
SALT	2 tablespoons	3. Refrigerate one hour to marinate cabbage in dressing. Turn cabbage over occasionally to marinate evenly.
WHITE PEPPER	1 teaspoon	
POWDERED MUSTARD	1 teaspoon	
SUGAR	2 teaspoons	

VARIATIONS OF BASIC SLAW

Slaw Variation	Subtract	Add	And/Or
TECHNICOLOR SLAW	1¾ pounds cabbage	2 cups radish slices, 2 cups carrot strips, 2 cups green or red pepper strips, 1 cup diced onions	
RADISH COLE SLAW	1¾ pounds cabbage	1¾ quarts radish slices	
RED AND WHITE SLAW			For cabbage use: 3½ pounds white cabbage, 3½ pounds red cabbage

GRAPE SLAW	1¾ pounds cabbage	1¾ quarts halved, seeded red grapes	
NUT SLAW			Sprinkle 1 tablespoon chopped nuts on each portion of basic slaw
SAVORY SLAW DELUXE	1¾ pounds cabbage, mayonnaise, lemon juice and seasonings	1¾ quarts green pepper strips	Toss with 1½ cups oil and vinegar dressing mixed with 3 tablespoons caraway seeds
SPICY FRUIT SLAW	3 pounds cabbage	2 quarts fresh pineapple slivers, 1 quart chopped parsley	Sprinkle a little crushed red pepper over top of each portion
CITRUS SLAW			Garnish each portion of basic slaw with 2-3 sections of orange
ROSY SLAW	1½ cups mayonnaise, 1/3 cup lemon juice	2 cups diced onions, 1½ cups sour cream	Top each portion with a radish rose
FRUITED SLAW	3½ pounds cabbage	1½ quarts orange slices, 1 quart diced apples, 1 quart pineapple chunks	

(cont.)

VARIATIONS OF BASIC COLE SLAW (Cont.)

Slaw Variation	Subtract	Add	And/Or
RAINBOW SLAW	2 pounds cabbage	1 quart finely shredded carrots, 1 quart finely sliced green peppers	For cabbage use: 2½ pounds green cabbage, 2½ pounds red cabbage
PEPPER SLAW			Garnish each portion of basic slaw with 2 green pepper rings
MEXICAN SLAW	3 pounds cabbage	1½ quarts onion rings, 1½ quarts of orange sections	Garnish each portion with sprigs of parsley
APPLE 'N GRAPE SLAW	3 pounds cabbage	2 cups chopped nuts; 1 quart halved, seeded grapes, 1½ quarts apple wedges	
GRAPE 'N CARROT SLAW	3 pounds cabbage	1 quart halved, seeded grapes, 2 quarts carrot strips	

RED, WHITE AND GREEN SLAW			For cabbage use: 3½ pounds red cabbage, 3½ pounds green cabbage Garnish each portion generously with chopped parsley
DUTCH SLAW	1½ cups mayonnaise, 1/3 cup lemon juice	1½ cups sour cream, 1/3 cup poppy seeds	
CARROT SLAW	3½ pounds cabbage	3½ quarts shredded carrots	
WILTED CABBAGE SLAW	Mayonnaise, lemon juice and seasonings	2 cups hot oil and vinegar dressing	Garnish with chopped parsley
RAISIN-APPLE SLAW	3 pounds cabbage	1 quart raisins, 2 quarts sliced apples	

MEXICAN SLAW WITH SPECIAL DRESSING

Yield: 20 portions

Ingredients

CABBAGE, shredded	4 pounds
SUGAR	2 ounces
SALT	1 tablespoon
GREEN PEPPERS, chopped	3 ounces
PIMIENTOES, chopped	2
SLAW DRESSING*	as needed

Procedure
1. Mix cabbage, sugar, salt, green peppers and pimientoes.
2. Add slaw dressing to moisten. Toss to mix.

*SLAW DRESSING

Yield: Approximately 5 quarts

Ingredients

MAYONNAISE	1 gallon
VINEGAR	1 quart
GARLIC POWDER	1 tablespoon
SUGAR	10 ounces
SALT	1 ounce

Procedure
1. Combine ingredients; mix well. Chill.

SPECIAL COLESLAW ⟶

Yield: 50 ½-cup portions

Ingredients

SALAD DRESSING	1 quart
VINEGAR	1 cup
CREAM, LIGHT	2 cups
MUSTARD, PREPARED	1½ tablespoons
SALT	1½ tablespoons
SEASONED SALT	1 tablespoon
CABBAGE, shredded	7½ pounds

PINEAPPLE COLESLAW

Yield: 40 portions (No. 10 scoop)

Ingredients

CABBAGE, shredded	1 gallon
SALT	1 tablespoon
SUGAR	1 tablespoon
PINEAPPLE, CRUSHED, drained	1 quart
RAISINS, chopped	1 cup
APPLES, chopped	1 cup
LEMON JUICE	½ cup
SOUR CREAM	¾ cup
SUGAR	½ cup

Procedure

1. Sprinkle cabbage with salt and sugar; toss together until thoroughly mixed.

2. Combine pineapple, raisins, apples and lemon juice; add to cabbage.

3. Blend sour cream and sugar, pour over salad mixture. Toss lightly until mixed.

Procedure

1. Blend salad dressing, vinegar and cream. Add mustard, salt and seasoned salt; mix well. Chill.

2. Combine the shredded cabbage with the salad dressing mixture. Serve on lettuce.

FRUITED CABBAGE SLAW

Yield: 24 ½-cup portions

Ingredients

GREEN CABBAGE, finely shredded	1 gallon
SEEDLESS GRAPES or GOLDEN RAISINS	2 cups
RED APPLES, unpeeled, diced	2 cups
SUGAR	1/3 cup
SALT	4 teaspoons
CARAWAY or CELERY SEEDS	2 teaspoons
LEMON JUICE or VINEGAR	2 tablespoons
LEMON RIND, grated	1/2 teaspoon
PREPARED MUSTARD	2 teaspoons
SOUR CREAM	1 to 1-1/4 cups

Procedure

1. Combine cabbage, grapes and apples.

2. Combine sugar, salt, caraway seeds, lemon juice and rind, mustard and sour cream; blend well.

3. Pour dressing over cabbage mixture. Toss with two spoons to mix well. Chill several hours to blend flavors.

SWEET-SOUR CABBAGE SLAW

Yield: 24 portions

Ingredients

CABBAGE, finely shredded	3 quarts
ONIONS, grated	¼ cup
CELERY SALT	2 teaspoons
SUGAR	¼ cup
VINEGAR	¼ cup
SALT	1 teaspoon
CAYENNE	½ teaspoon
HEAVY CREAM, whipped or THICK SOUR CREAM	2 cups

Procedure

1. Combine cabbage, onions and celery salt.

2. Blend the remaining ingredients; pour over the cabbage; toss lightly to mix.

RAISIN APPLE SLAW

Yield: 24 portions

Ingredients

MAYONNAISE	1-1/2 cups
SOUR CREAM	1-1/2 cups
VINEGAR	1/3 cup
SALT	as needed
MUSTARD (optional)	2 teaspoons
CHEESE, AMERICAN, grated	1 cup
RAISINS, LIGHT OR DARK	2 to 3 cups
CABBAGE, shredded	3 quarts
APPLES, unpeeled, sliced or diced	3 to 4 large

Procedure

1. Combine mayonnaise, sour cream, vinegar, salt, mustard and cheese.

2. Rinse raisins; dry thoroughly.

3. Combine raisins, cabbage and apple slices. Add dressing; toss lightly to mix. Serve on crisp salad greens, if desired.

TOSSED FRUIT SLAW

Yield: 25 portions

Ingredients

CABBAGE, shredded	1¼ pounds
LETTUCE, shredded	1½ quarts
RAISINS, washed	1 cup
ORANGES, diced	6
SLICED PINEAPPLE, CANNED, drained, diced	2½ cups
SALT	1½ teaspoons
FRUIT FRENCH DRESSING (pp. 198, 206)	¾ cup

Procedure

1. Combine cabbage, lettuce, raisins, oranges and pineapple. Chill.

2. Add salt to French dressing. Just before serving pour dressing over salad ingredients; toss lightly to mix.

Note

Diced bananas may be substituted for part of orange or pineapple. Add just before combining with dressing.

JADE COLESLAW

Yield: 100 portions

Ingredients

SYRUP FROM CANNED CLING PEACHES	1 cup
VINEGAR, CIDER	¾ cup
CELERY SEEDS	1 teaspoon
GREEN BEANS, BLUE LAKE, cut, drained	1 No. 10 can
CLING PEACHES, sliced, drained	1 quart
CABBAGE, shredded	8¼ pounds
ONIONS, finely chopped	¼ cup
PEPPER, WHITE	¼ teaspoon
CELERY SALT	1 tablespoon
SALT	2 teaspoons
SALAD DRESSING	3 cups

Procedure

1. Combine syrup, vinegar and celery seeds; pour over drained beans. Marinate, refrigerated, for about 1 hour.

2. Cut peach slices into fourths.

3. Combine cabbage, peaches and marinated green beans. Toss gently.

4. Add onions and seasonings to salad dressing. Pour over cabbage mixture; toss to mix.

5. Chill slaw 1 hour before serving.

WILLIAM TELL SLAW ⟶

Yield: 48 portions (½ cup)

Ingredients

SALAD DRESSING	1-1/2 quarts
LEMON JUICE	1/3 cup
INSTANT ONIONS, finely rolled	2 tablespoons
SALT	1 tablespoon
PEPPER, WHITE	1/2 teaspoon
APPLES, RED-SKINNED, quartered, cored	2 pounds
AMERICAN CHEESE, grated	3 pounds
CABBAGE, shredded medium-fine	5 pounds

MEXICAN SLAW

Yield: 16 5-ounce portions

Ingredients

KIDNEY BEANS, canned	2 pounds
CELERY, sliced in ¼-inch crescents	12 ounces
CABBAGE, shredded	1 pound
CHEESE, sliced, cut in ½-inch squares	8 ounces
SWEET PICKLE RELISH	4 ounces
MAYONNAISE	8 ounces
SALT	1½ teaspoons
WORCESTERSHIRE SAUCE	1 teaspoon
LIQUID HOT PEPPER SEASONING	3 drops
VINEGAR	1 tablespoon

Procedure

1. Rinse beans; drain thoroughly. Combine with celery, cabbage, cheese and relish.
2. Mix mayonnaise with remaining ingredients.
3. Just before serving, pour dressing over vegetable mixture; toss lightly to mix.

Note

When multiplying recipe, combine in 16-portion batches, mixing 4 pounds, 8 ounces vegetable mixture with 1 cup dressing.

Procedure

1. Combine salad dressing, lemon juice, onions, salt and pepper.
2. Dice or slice apple quarters into dressing, stirring often to coat well.
3. Add cheese and cabbage; mix lightly but thoroughly. Chill.
4. Serve on crisp salad greens.

Rice Salads

Rice Council

Rice and Macaroni Salads

FLAVORFUL salads prepared with rice or macaroni make a welcome addition to the luncheon menu. As hearty salads— the type with a real satiety value—you can present them with a simple garnish on a bed of crisp greens. Or, you can feature them as a cold plate attraction, escorted by cold meats, deviled eggs or sliced cheese.

Neutral in both color and taste, rice and macaroni readily accept the zest of seasonings and the bright flashes of color contributed by vegetables. For best results, have the rice fluffy and dry, the macaroni cooked until just tender and thoroughly drained. Add the seasoned dressing to the cooked rice or macaroni while it is still warm. And, after all of the ingredients are added and the salad is mixed, allow enough time to permit the flavors to mingle and "become acquainted."

ASPARAGUS AND RICE SALAD

Yield: 12 portions

Ingredients

OIL AND VINEGAR DRESSING	1 cup
DILL WEED	½ teaspoon
ONION, minced	¼ cup
RICE, cooked, hot	1½ quarts
PEAS, cooked	2 cups
CARROTS, shredded	½ cup
CELERY, sliced	2 cups
TOMATOES, medium, diced	4
SALT	1 teaspoon
PEPPER	½ teaspoon
ASPARAGUS SPEARS, cooked	24

Procedure

1. Combine dressing, dill weed and onion. Pour over hot rice; mix lightly. Cool to room temperature.

2. Add peas, carrots, celery, tomatoes, salt and pepper. Toss lightly to mix. Adjust seasoning, if necessary. Chill.

3. Serve salad on crisp greens. Arrange asparagus spears on top of salad. Serve with additional oil and vinegar dressing, as desired.

MACARONI AND CHEESE SALAD ⟶

Yield: 15 portions

Ingredients

ELBOW MACARONI, cooked	1 quart
SALT	1 teaspoon
CELERY SALT	1 teaspoon
SWEET RELISH	1/3 cup
PIMIENTOES, chopped	1/4 cup
CELERY, sliced	1 cup
AMERICAN CHEESE, processed, sharp, diced	1 cup
EGGS, hard-cooked, chopped	3
MAYONNAISE	2 cups

RICE SUPPER SALAD

Yield: 50 portions

Ingredients

RICE, cooked	1-1/2 quarts
FRENCH DRESSING	1 cup
SALT	4 teaspoons
PEPPER	1 teaspoon
ONIONS, minced	1 cup
CELERY, chopped	2-1/2 cups
GREEN PEPPERS, chopped	1-1/2 cups
PIMIENTOES, chopped	2/3 cup
PICKLES, SOUR OR DILL, minced	1 cup
SWEET RELISH	2/3 cup
EGGS, hard-cooked, chopped	12
MAYONNAISE	2-1/2 cups

Procedure

1. Combine rice, French dressing, salt, pepper and onions; let stand while preparing other ingredients.

2. Add remaining ingredients; mix thoroughly. Chill well. Serve as a starch salad with frankfurters or cold meats. Garnish top of salad with sliced hard-cooked eggs, if desired.

Procedure

1. Combine macaroni with all ingredients except mayonnaise. Mix well.

2. Add mayonnaise and toss lightly.

3. Serve on a lettuce leaf. Add parsley garnish.

MACARONI SALAD

Yield: 24 portions

Ingredients

MACARONI, SALAD CUT	1 pound, 8 ounces
WATER	as needed
SALT	as needed
CELERY, chopped	1 pound, 8 ounces
GREEN ONIONS, chopped	6 ounces
PIMIENTOES, chopped	6 ounces
GREEN PEPPERS, chopped	6 ounces
PARSLEY, chopped	1 ounce
SWEET PICKLE RELISH, drained	8 ounces
MAYONNAISE	3 cups
LEMON JUICE	3 tablespoons
TARRAGON VINEGAR	3 tablespoons
WORCESTERSHIRE SAUCE	1 tablespoon
SALT	1 tablespoon
PEPPER, WHITE	1 teaspoon
MUSTARD, DRY	½ teaspoon

Procedure

1. Cook macaroni in boiled salted water. Drain. Rinse; drain again.

2. Combine macaroni, celery, green onions, pimiento, green pepper, parsley and relish. (All ingredients should be well drained.)

3. Combine mayonnaise and seasonings; mix well. Pour over macaroni mixture; mix lightly but thoroughly.

Variation

For Macaroni and Bacon Salad, dice 8 ounces bacon into ½-inch pieces. Cook slowly until done but not crisp. Add bacon to macaroni with vegetables (step 2 above).

Macaroni Salad Go-Togethers

General Foods Corp.

PINEAPPLE MACARONI SALAD

Yield: 100 ½-cup portions

Ingredients

MACARONI, SALAD CUT	2¾ pounds
WATER, boiling	2 gallons
SALT	½ cup
PINEAPPLE TIDBITS, thoroughly drained	1 No. 10 can
GREEN PEPPERS or CELERY, chopped	1½ pounds
DILL PICKLE, chopped	1 pound, 14 ounces
GREEN ONIONS, chopped	8 ounces
CHEESE, CHEDDAR, diced	1½ pounds
MAYONNAISE	1¼ quarts
SEASONED SALT	3 tablespoons
DILL WEED	1 tablespoon

Procedure

1. Cook macaroni in boiling water with first amount of salt until barely tender, about 10 minutes. Drain; rinse with cold water. Cool.

2. Combine macaroni, pineapple, green pepper (or celery), pickle, onion and cheese.

3. Combine mayonnaise, seasoned salt and dill weed. Add to macaroni mixture. Toss lightly to mix. Chill.

4. Serve on crisp salad greens.

CHEDDAR-MAC SALAD

Yield: 24 ¾-cup portions

Ingredients

MACARONI, ELBOW, uncooked	14 ounces
PEAS, FROZEN	20 ounces
CHEESE, CHEDDAR, cubed	1 pound
CELERY, chopped	1 cup
ONIONS, chopped	2/3 cup
SOUR CREAM	1-3/4 cups
VINEGAR	1 tablespoon
SALT	1 tablespoon
SUGAR	1 tablespoon
MUSTARD, PREPARED	1/2 teaspoon
MILK	1/2 cup

Procedure

1. Cook macaroni according to package directions; chill.
2. Cook peas until just tender; chill.
3. Combine macaroni, peas, cheese, celery and onion.
4. Blend sour cream, vinegar, salt, sugar and mustard. Gradually stir in milk.
5. Pour dressing over macaroni mixture; toss lightly to mix. Chill several hours to blend flavors.

Salad Plates with Pears

Pacific Coast Canned Pear Service Inc.

FRUIT SALADS

MANY refreshing salads can be created with fruit, both fresh and canned. To make them, cut-up fruits may be mixed together lightly and spooned onto greens. Or, whole fruits or sizable pieces may be arranged in an eye-catching pattern or placed in colorful groupings.

For the greatest salad success, use only top quality fruit. Select fresh fruit that is ripe—but not too ripe—and canned fruit that is firm and perfectly shaped.

To keep the surfaces of cut fresh fruits from turning dark, prepare as near serving time as possible. Dip at once into pineapple, grapefruit, orange, lemon or lime juice. Or, use one of the ascorbic or citric acid preparations that are available to keep fruit from discoloring.

One of the most popular fruit salad mixtures is the Waldorf, a combination of apples, celery, nutmeats and mayonnaise dressing. It's a salad that lends itself easily to variation by omitting the nuts and adding in their place plumped raisins, pineapple chunks, halved and seeded grapes, julienne strips of dates, diced canned peaches or segments of orange. Still another version without nuts calls for sprinkling portions of the salad with shredded sharp cheddar cheese.

Colorful mixtures of cut fruits make a handsome presentation when piled in a pineapple shell or atop a broad wedge of honeydew melon. Similar fruit mixtures spark the inspiration for frozen fruit salads.

Some fruits—prunes, peaches, apricots and pears—lend themselves to stuffing with cheese. Avocado halves or rings make delightful "containers" for citrus sections. Other fruits, chosen for firmness, color and size, make an impressive novelty when strung on a skewer.

Several fruits arranged as a salad plate combine in pleasing fashion with cottage cheese, scoops of sherbet, or cream cheese balls rolled in chopped nuts. These large salads team happily on the menu with sandwiches of nut or fruit breads for a "light" noontime meal or a hearty evening snack.

STUFFED PRUNE AND GRAPEFRUIT SALAD

Yield: 24 portions, 3 prunes, 9 grapefruit sections each

Ingredients

PRUNES, large, cooked	72
CREAM CHEESE	1 pound
COTTAGE CHEESE, sieved	1 pound
LIGHT CREAM	as needed
FILBERTS, chopped	1 cup
GRAPEFRUIT, sectioned	18
LETTUCE	as needed
CRESS	24 sprigs

Procedure

1. Drain prunes. Remove pits, spread apart and place on trays lined with paper towels.

2. Blend cream and cottage cheeses, moistening with light cream as necessary.

3. Use pastry bag to fill prunes with a large rosette of cheese. Sprinkle cheese with chopped filberts.

4. To arrange salad: place three groups of grapefruit sections on lettuce using three sections of fruit in each group. Place a stuffed prune between each group of grapefruit. Garnish with cress.

PACIFIC AVOCADO SALAD

Yield: 1 portion

Ingredients

AVOCADO SLICES	5
GRAPEFRUIT SECTIONS	5
RIBIER GRAPES or RIPE OLIVES	5
SALAD GREENS	

Procedure

1. Sprinkle avocado slices with lemon juice and salt.

2. Arrange avocado slices on salad greens alternately with grapefruit. Center with grapes or pitted ripe olives.

3. Serve with French Dressing.

COTTAGE CHEESE AND CRANBERRY RIBBON SALAD

Yield: 16 portions, ½ cup cheese, ¼ cup cranberries

Ingredients

CRANBERRIES, FRESH	1 pound
SUGAR	2 cups
WATER	1 cup
COTTAGE CHEESE	2 quarts (4 pounds)

Procedure

1. Rinse berries; drain.
2. Combine with sugar and water in a deep saucepan. Heat to boiling point, stirring until sugar dissolves.
3. Cover; reduce heat. Boil gently 5 minutes. Remove from heat; let set 5 minutes.
4. Return to heat; cook for another 5 minutes. Cool; refrigerate overnight. This produces a thick sparkling red whole cranberry sauce.
5. To make salads, line salad plate with chicory or other crisp salad greens. Spoon on cottage cheese dropping from side of spoon to make a narrow strip. Make two parallel strips of the cheese allowing space between. Spoon whole cranberry sauce down the center.

FRUITED COTTAGE CHEESE ⟶

Yield: 1½ gallons

Ingredients

PINEAPPLE TIDBITS, drained	2 pounds
ORANGES, ½-inch dice, drained	2 pounds
APPLES, unpeeled, ½-inch dice	2 pounds
COTTAGE CHEESE	5 pounds
MAYONNAISE	2 cups
SALT	2 teaspoons

Fruit Arranged with Cottage Cheese

California Prune Advisory Board

Procedure

1. Combine thoroughly-drained fruit with cottage cheese, mayonnaise and salt.

2. Serve as a relish or on lettuce as a salad. Or, use to stuff avocado half.

Note

Drained diced peaches, diced bananas and chopped celery or other combinations may also be used. Substitute by weight. Always include some tart crisp fruit.

GRAPE WALDORF SALAD

Yield: 30 portions

Ingredients

APPLES, cut (see procedure)	1 gallon
MAYONNAISE	4 cups
VINEGAR	¼ cup
CELERY, coarsely sliced	1½ quarts
TOKAY GRAPES, halved and seeded	3 cups
LETTUCE, shredded	7 quarts
PECANS, chopped	1¼ cups
MARASCHINO CHERRIES	15

Procedure

1. Wash apples. Put 2 cups of the mayonnaise and the vinegar into gallon container. Cut apples into large bite size pieces into mayonnaise and stir often so apples will not discolor.

2. When gallon is filled, pour into large bowl. Add celery and grapes and rest of mayonnaise and toss well.

3. Fill lettuce lined soup bowls with scant cup full of shredded lettuce. Portion apple mixture on top of lettuce. Garnish each portion with two teaspoons cut pecans and half a cherry.

ZESTY CITRUS SALAD

Yield: 25 ¾-cup portions

Ingredients

GRAPEFRUIT SECTIONS	2 quarts
ORANGE SECTIONS	2 quarts
ONIONS, SWEET, thinly sliced	2 cups
LETTUCE	3 heads
PARSLEY, chopped	½ cup

Procedure

1. Combine grapefruit and orange sections; drain.

2. Separate onion slices into rings. Place in citrus juice; refrigerate to crisp onions.

3. Arrange fruit in lettuce cups. Garnish with onion rings and chopped parsley.

4. Serve with Fruit French dressing (pp. 198 and 206).

SALAD SOPHISTICATE

Yield: 24 portions

Ingredients

AVOCADOS	12
LEMON JUICE	¼ cup
SALT	as needed
PINEAPPLE CHUNKS, chilled	1½ quarts
MARASCHINO CHERRIES, quartered	18
ROQUEFORT DRESSING	3 cups

Procedure

1. Cut each avocado into halves length-wise. Remove seed; sprinkle with lemon juice and salt.

2. Arrange on crisp salad greens. Fill with pineapple. Cut cherries in quarters. Garnish each portion with 3 pieces of cherry. Serve with Roquefort dressing.

FIESTA FRUIT PLATE

Yield: 1 portion

Ingredients

LETTUCE	as needed
CLING PEACH HALF	1
AVOCADO SLICES	3
APRICOT HALVES, canned	2
PEAR HALF, canned	1
BANANA CHUNKS*	3
GRAPES, jubilee style	5 grapes
LIME or MINT SHERBET	No. 16 scoop
MINT	sprig

Procedure

1. Line chilled plate with lettuce. Arrange a bed of shredded lettuce.

2. Arrange peach half, avocado slices, apricot halves, pear half and banana chunks in a circle on plate.

3. Fill pear half with grapes.

4. Place scoop of sherbet in center. Garnish with mint.

*Cut from whole banana spread with mayonnaise and rolled in chopped walnuts.

AVOCADO CONTINENTAL SALAD

Yield: 48 portions

Ingredients

CREAM CHEESE, softened	3 pounds
EGG YOLKS	16
LEMON JUICE	1 cup
PEPPER, WHITE	½ teaspoon
PAPRIKA	½ teaspoon
AVOCADOS, large, ripe	24
LEMON JUICE	as needed
SALAD GREENS	as needed
CHIPPED BEEF, finely chopped	1½ pounds

Procedure

1. Beat cream cheese until fluffy. Add egg yolks, one at a time, beating well after each addition.

2. Blend in lemon juice and seasonings. Heat in double boiler over hot water. Cool. Chill.

3. Quarter avocados, remove seeds. Peel; brush with lemon juice.

4. For each portion, arrange two quarters of avocado on salad greens. Sprinkle avocado with chipped beef.

5. Spoon cream cheese sauce over top. Garnish with cress, if desired.

RAISIN WALDORF SALAD

Yield: 24 ½-cup portions

Ingredients

RAISINS, LIGHT or DARK	2 cups
CELERY, chopped	1 quart
APPLES, diced	2 quarts
WALNUTS, broken	1½ cups
SALAD DRESSING	1 cup
LEMON JUICE, FRESH	¼ cup
SALT	1 teaspoon

Procedure

1. Rinse raisins; drain thoroughly. Combine with celery, apples and walnuts.

2. Blend salad dressing, lemon juice and salt; mix lightly with salad.

Sunny Fruit Salad

Cling Peach Advisory Board

SUNNY FRUIT SALAD

Yield: 1 portion

Ingredients

ROMAINE LEAVES	4 to 5
CANNED CLING PEACH SLICES	7
GRAPEFRUIT SECTIONS, large	2
AVOCADO SLICES	2
BANANA SLICES	4
CREAM CHEESE, whipped	1 ounce
MARASCHINO CHERRY on stem	1

Procedure

1. Line a salad plate with romaine, arranging leaves parallel to each other.

2. Place peach slices within romaine leaf toward one side of the plate.

3. Arrange grapefruit and avocado in center portion of the plate and place the banana slices in a group toward the side of the plate opposite from the peaches.

4. Spoon the whipped cream cheese next to the peach slices.

5. Garnish with the cherry, placing it with the grapefruit in the center of the arrangement.

SLICED ORANGE SALAD—POPPY SEED DRESSING

Yield: 1 portion

Ingredients

ORANGE, medium to large, peeled and sliced into 5 slices	1
ONION RINGS, small	3

Procedure

1. Arrange orange slices on shredded lettuce bed on salad plate lined with leaf lettuce. Top with onion rings.
2. Pour 2 tablespoons Poppy Seed Dressing* on top.

*POPPY SEED DRESSING

Yield: 3½ cups, 28 portions

Ingredients

SUGAR	1-1/2 cups
DRY MUSTARD	2 teaspoons
SALT	2 teaspoons
VINEGAR	2/3 cup
ONION JUICE	3 tablespoons
SALAD OIL	2 cups
POPPY SEEDS	3 tablespoons

Procedure

1. Mix sugar, mustard, salt and vinegar.
2. Add onion juice.
3. Add salad oil slowly, beating constantly. Add poppy seeds.

FOUR SEASONS SALAD WITH CHERVIL DRESSING

Yield: 50 portions

Ingredients

ROMAINE LEAVES	100
STRAWBERRIES, FROZEN WHOLE, partially thawed	1 6½-pound package
PINEAPPLE CHUNKS, drained	1 No. 10 can
AVOCADOS, ripe, cut into balls	4
MELON BALLS, FROZEN partially thawed, drained	2 pounds
PEACH SLICES, drained	½ No. 10 can

Dressing

VINEGAR, WHITE WINE	1 quart
OLIVE OIL	1 quart
SUGAR	4 ounces
CHERVIL	3 tablespoons
NUTMEG	1 tablespoon
ORANGE RIND, grated	1 tablespoon
MARJORAM	½ tablespoon
LEMON RIND, grated	½ tablespoon

Procedure

1. Arrange romaine leaves in tall stemmed glasses.

2. Combine fruits; fill glasses.

3. To make dressing, combine ingredients; shake or beat thoroughly to mix. Pour over fruits.

Kebab Salad

California Prune Advisory Board

KEBAB SALAD

Yield: 48 portions

Ingredients

PRUNES, large, dried, with pits	3 pounds
OR plumped, with pits	4½ pounds
OR plumped, pitted	3 pounds, 10 ounces
ORANGES, large	6
APPLES, RED, large	6
LEMON JUICE or other anti-oxidant	as needed
BANANAS, large	6
SALAD GREENS	as needed
MINT	48 sprigs

Procedure

1. If using dried prunes, cover with cold water; bring to a boil. Reduce heat. Cover; simmer 10 minutes. Cool. Drain.

2. Cut each unpeeled orange into 8 wedges.

3. Cut apples into 8 wedges. Remove core; do not pare. Coat with lemon juice.

4. Peel bananas. Cut each into 8 chunks. Coat with lemon juice.

5. Thread one piece of each of the 4 fruits on a skewer. Arrange on crisp salad greens. Garnish with mint.

STUFFED PRUNE SALAD

Yield: 8 portions

Ingredients

PRUNES, cooked, seeded	40
CREAM CHEESE MIXTURE*	1¼ pounds
LETTUCE CUPS	8
MARSHMALLOWS, cut in half	4
MARASCHINO CHERRY RINGS	8
PECANS, chopped, toasted	1 tablespoon

Procedure

1. Fill prunes with cream cheese mixture using pastry bag with star tube. Allow ½ ounce of mixture per prune.

2. For each salad, arrange 5 prunes on lettuce, wheel fashion. Place ½ marshmallow in center. Garnish with a cherry ring. Sprinkle chopped toasted pecans over top of prunes.

*CREAM CHEESE MIXTURE

Yield: 3 pounds

Ingredients

COTTAGE CHEESE	2 pounds
CREAM CHEESE (at room temperature)	14 ounces
SALT	1 teaspoon
CREAM, whipped	1 ounce (¼ cup)
MAYONNAISE	1 ounce (2 table-spoons)

Procedure

1. Mix cottage cheese smooth in bowl of chopping machine (or force through a ricer; run through a food mill; or put through a grinder, using finest plate).

2. Add cream cheese and salt; mix until smooth.

3. Fold whipped cream and mayonnaise together; add to cheese.

FROZEN FRUIT SALAD I

Yield: 96 portions

Ingredients

PINEAPPLE TIDBITS	3 quarts
PEACHES, diced	3 quarts
WHITE GRAPES	2 quarts
PEARS, diced	2 quarts
MANDARIN ORANGE SEGMENTS	2 quarts
MARASCHINO CHERRIES	3 cups
MINIATURE MARSHMALLOWS	2 quarts
COCONUT	3 cups
ORANGE or PINEAPPLE JUICE	2 cups
LEMON JUICE	½ cup
MAYONNAISE	1 quart
FRUIT SALAD DRESSING*	1 gallon, 2½ quarts

Procedure

1. Drain fruits.

2. Combine fruits, marshmallows, coconut, orange juice, lemon juice and mayonnaise.

3. Fold in fruit salad dressing.

4. Line three 12-inch by 20-inch by 2½-inch pans with foil. Pour fruit mixture into pans. Seal, label and freeze.

5. When frozen, remove pan; stack sealed packages together.

*FRUIT SALAD DRESSING ⟶

Yield: 2¼ gallons

Ingredients

PINEAPPLE or ORANGE JUICE	2 quarts
LEMON JUICE	1 cup
SUGAR	2 pounds (4½ cups)
CORNSTARCH	1 cup
SALT	2 teaspoons
LEMON RIND, grated	2 tablespoons
EGGS, slightly beaten	24
CREAM, WHIPPING	2 quarts

Maraschino Cherries Spark Frozen Fruit Salad

National Cherry Growers & Industries Foundation

Procedure

1. Combine pineapple and lemon juice; heat in double boiler or steam jacket kettle.

2. Mix sugar, cornstarch, salt and lemon rind. Stir into hot liquid; cook until thickened, stirring constantly.

3. Stir part of the hot mixture into beaten eggs. Add egg mixture to portion of thickened fruit juice remaining in double boiler. Cook and stir until smooth. Cool.

4. Whip cream; fold into cooled mixture.

FROZEN FRUIT SALAD II

Yield: 17½ pounds, 72 portions

Ingredients

CREAM CHEESE, softened	1 pound
MAYONNAISE	2-1/2 cups
LEMON JUICE	2/3 cup
SALT	1/2 teaspoon
SUGAR	2/3 cup
PINEAPPLE TIDBITS, drained	2-1/2 pounds
MANDARIN ORANGE SECTIONS, drained	2-1/2 pounds
PRUNES, PLUMPED, quartered	5-1/4 pounds
MARASCHINO CHERRIES, quartered	1 pound
PECANS, chopped	14 ounces
CREAM, HEAVY (for whipping)*	1-1/4 quarts

Procedure

1. Blend softened cheese, mayonnaise, lemon juice, salt and sugar.

2. Combine drained fruits and pecans; fold into cream cheese mixture.

3. Whip cream; lightly fold into fruit and cheese mixture.

4. Pour into two 12-inch by 20-inch by 2-inch pans. Cover tightly with freezer wrap or foil; freeze.

5. Unmold by quickly dipping pan in hot water. Cut into squares. Arrange on lettuce, chicory or cress.

*Or 2½ quarts prepared whipped topping.

FROZEN FRUIT SALAD IV

Yield: 48 portions

Ingredients

EGG YOLKS, beaten	12 (1 cup)
SUGAR	¾ cup
VINEGAR, TARRAGON	¾ cup
CREAM, HEAVY	2½ quarts
PINEAPPLE, CRUSHED, drained	4½ cups
NUTS, coarsely chopped	3 cups
BANANAS, mashed	3

FROZEN FRUIT SALAD III

Yield: 48 4-ounce portions

Ingredients

EVAPORATED MILK or HEAVY CREAM	1 quart
GELATINE, unflavored	2 tablespoons
WATER, cold	¾ cup
CREAM CHEESE, softened	1 pound
LEMON or LIME JUICE	1 cup
SALT	1½ teaspoons
MAYONNAISE	1½ cups
BANANAS, diced	1½ quarts
ORANGES, diced	1½ quarts
MARASCHINO CHERRIES, diced	¾ cup

Procedure

1. Chill evaporated milk in freezing compartment until almost frozen.

2. Soften gelatine in cold water; dissolve over low heat.

3. Blend softened cream cheese, lemon juice, salt and mayonnaise.

4. Whip chilled milk or heavy cream in a chilled bowl until stiff. Stir in dissolved gelatine. Combine with cheese mixture; fold in the diced fruit.

5. Pile in 4 ounce souffle cups. Place in freezer immediately; freeze until firm.

6. Defrost at room temperature 15-20 minutes before serving. Serve on a generous bed of watercress.

Procedure

1. Cook egg yolks, sugar and vinegar in double boiler until thickened, stirring. Cool.

2. Whip cream until stiff; fold into cooled mixture. Fold in drained pineapple, nuts and bananas.

3. Turn mixture into loaf pans or 4-ounce paper cups (which may be peeled off when ready to serve). Freeze several hours.

4. Serve in lettuce cups garnished with sprigs of watercress and a cherry slice. Serve with whipped cream dressing or mayonnaise, if desired.

FROZEN FRUIT SALAD V

Yield: 3 gallons, 96 ½-cup portions

Ingredients

GELATIN, LEMON	1½ pounds
SALT	1½ teaspoons
FRUIT JUICE AND WATER, hot	3 quarts
LEMON JUICE	1 cup
MAYONNAISE or SOUR CREAM	1 quart
DICED ASSORTED FRUIT*, drained	1½ gallons
CREAM, HEAVY	1½ quarts

Procedure

1. Dissolve gelatin and salt in hot liquid. Add lemon juice and mayonnaise; mix with whip until blended. Chill until slightly thickened.
2. Fold in fruit.
3. Whip cream to soft peaks; fold into fruit mixture.
4. Turn into loaf pans; freeze until firm.
5. Remove from freezer 20 minutes before serving.
6. Cut into slices; serve on crisp greens.

*Any desired assortment of canned, fresh or frozen fruit may be used, except fresh or frozen pineapple. Sweeten fresh fruit before adding.

APPLE, PINEAPPLE AND NUT SALAD

Yield: 3 quarts

Ingredients

PINEAPPLE, CRUSHED	1 cup
APPLES, diced	5 pounds
CELERY, finely sliced	1 quart
MAYONNAISE	2 cups
SALT	½ tablespoon
NUTS, pecan or walnut pieces	1¼ cups

Procedure

1. Drain pineapple. Sprinkle apples with pineapple juice to prevent discoloration. Add celery.
2. Combine mayonnaise, crushed pineapple and salt. Blend well.
3. Pour over apple-celery mixture. Toss lightly to mix.
4. Serve in a Boston lettuce cup or on shredded lettuce. Sprinkle the top with nuts.

PEACH WALDORF SALAD

Yield: 6 quarts, 48 ½-cup portions

Ingredients

APPLES, diced	2 quarts
CELERY, diced	2 quarts
RAISINS or DATE PIECES	2 cups
SALAD DRESSING	2 cups
LEMON JUICE	½ cup
SALT	2 teaspoons
CLING PEACHES, sliced, drained	1 No. 10 can

Procedure

1. Combine apples, celery and raisins.
2. Blend salad dressing, lemon juice and salt. Pour over apple mixture; toss lightly.
3. Just before serving, add well drained peach slices; mix very lightly. Serve on crisp salad greens.

INDIO FRUIT SALAD

Yield: 24 portions

Ingredients

BACON, thinly sliced	1 pound
DATES, FRESH	1 quart
CELERY, sliced	1 quart
BANANAS, sliced	8 medium
SOUR CREAM	2 cups
LEMON RIND, grated	2 teaspoons
LEMON JUICE	3 to 4 tablespoons
CURRY POWDER	1 teaspoon
SALT	¾ teaspoon
LETTUCE	as needed

Procedure

1. Cook bacon until crisp; drain well. Crumble.
2. Cut dates into mixing bowl. Add celery and bananas.
3. Combine sour cream, lemon rind, lemon juice, curry powder and salt; blend.
4. Pour dressing over fruit; toss lightly.
5. Serve in crisp lettuce cups. Top with crumbled bacon.

BANANA FINGERS AND ORANGE SALAD

Yield: 12 portions

Ingredients

BANANAS,	6
MAYONNAISE	1 ounce
PEANUTS, UNSALTED, SKINLESS, chopped	6 ounces
LETTUCE, 5-dozen size	1 ½ heads
ORANGES, 126 size, sliced	5-1/3 oranges (48 slices)
MARSHMALLOWS, cut in half	6
MARASCHINO CHERRY RINGS	12

Procedure

1. Peel bananas, cut off rounded tips, reserving for other fruit salads. Cut into halves crosswise.

2. Split each piece in half lengthwise. Coat pieces with mayonnaise. Cover with peanuts, using ½ ounce per portion (2 banana pieces).

3. Place on plate lined with lettuce, arranging with 4 slices of orange, wheel fashion. Place half a marshmallow in center of each salad. Garnish with cherry ring.

ORANGE WALDORF SALAD

Yield: 50 portions

Ingredients

APPLES, diced	1 gallon
LEMON JUICE	½ cup
SALT	1 tablespoon
SUGAR	¼ cup
CELERY, diced	2 quarts
ORANGES, diced	2 quarts
RAISINS or CHOPPED DATES	2 cups
MAYONNAISE	2 cups
WALNUT MEATS, chopped	1 cup

Procedure

1. Sprinkle apples with lemon juice, salt and sugar.

2. Combine apples, celery, oranges, raisins and mayonnaise. Chill.

3. Serve on crisp salad greens. Garnish with chopped walnut meats.

Wantagh Salad

Pacific Coast Canned Pear Service, Inc.

WANTAGH SALAD

Yield: 100 portions

Ingredients

MAYONNAISE	3 cups
LEMON JUICE	1 cup
SUGAR	1 cup
SALT	2 teaspoons
CELERY, chopped	1 gallon
WALNUTS, chopped	1 quart
RAISINS, SEEDLESS	1½ cups
BARTLETT PEAR HALVES, CANNED, drained, diced	3 gallons

Procedure
1. Combine mayonnaise, lemon juice, sugar and salt.
2. Add celery, walnuts and raisins; toss to mix.
3. Fold in diced canned pears; mix lightly.
4. Serve on crisp salad greens.

Small Fruit Salads

Cling Peach Advisory Board

WALDORF SALAD

Yield: 24 portions

Ingredients

APPLES, SIZE 80	12 (6 pounds)
PINEAPPLE JUICE	2 quarts
LEMON JUICE, from	1 lemon
SALT	2 teaspoons
CELERY, diced	1¼ pounds
SUGAR	4 teaspoons
MAYONNAISE	10 ounces
CREAM, whipped	2 ounces
LETTUCE	2 heads
PECANS, chopped	2½ ounces

Procedure

1. Peel and dice apples, dropping into mixture of pineapple juice, lemon juice and salt. Drain thoroughly. Combine with celery.

2. Add sugar to mayonnaise; fold in whipped cream. Pour dressing over apples and celery; toss lightly to mix.

3. Serve in lettuce cups allowing 4 ounces per portion. Garnish each portion with 1 teaspoon pecans.

PINK AMBROSIA FRUIT SALAD

Yield: 50 portions

Ingredients

MANDARIN ORANGE SECTIONS	3 quarts
PINEAPPLE CUBES	3 quarts
MARASCHINO CHERRIES, halved	3 cups
MINIATURE MARSHMALLOWS	3 quarts
STRAWBERRY YOGHURT	1 quart
SOUR CREAM	2 quarts
FLAKED COCONUT	1 quart
COCONUT	to garnish
MARASCHINO CHERRIES	to garnish

Procedure

1. Drain fruit thoroughly.

2. Combine fruit and marshmallows; fold in strawberry yoghurt and sour cream. Fold in coconut.

3. Chill, covered, in refrigerator overnight.

4. Serve in crisp lettuce cups. Garnish with additional coconut and maraschino cherries.

AMBROSIA SALAD

Yield: 2 gallons

Ingredients

PINEAPPLE CHUNKS, well drained	1 No. 10 can
MANDARIN ORANGE SEGMENTS, well drained	2 quarts
MINIATURE MARSHMALLOWS	1 quart
COCONUT, SHREDDED	1 cup
WHITE CREME DE CACAO	¼ cup
SALT	1 teaspoon
SOUR CREAM	2 quarts
COCONUT	to garnish
MARASCHINO CHERRY	to garnish

Procedure

1. Combine pineapple, orange segments, marshmallows, coconut and white creme de cacao. Toss together to mix.

2. Add salt to sour cream. Fold into fruit mixture. Refrigerate, covered, overnight.

3. Serve on lettuce. Garnish with additional coconut and a maraschino cherry.

A Bowlful of Dressings

SALAD DRESSINGS

THE BASIC dressings are few in number. But with simple
additions, the possibilities for new and exciting flavor interests
are almost endless. The established standbys—French dressing
and mayonnaise—are the foundations for any number of other
dressings. Commercial sour cream is another adaptable "basic."
And so is salad dressing, a ready-to-use product that combines
the smooth emulsified quality of mayonnaise with some of
the nippy flavor of old-fashioned boiled dressing.

You can create other dressings by blending two or more
dressings together. Combine mayonnaise with French, for in-
stance, for vegetable salads and to toss with slaws. Fold sour
cream into mayonnaise to use as a salad garnish and to toss
with salad mixtures. Sour cream "lightens" mayonnaise and
makes it less cloying. And another advantage: salads mixed
with this blend hold their fresh appearance longer.

It can hardly be expected that all salad dressings will con-
form to the basic dressing-plus-something-or-other plan. There
are many popular recipe-made versions that are not a direct
offspring of a standard preparation. Still other types of salad
dressing include the cooked dressings (often a piquant fruit

juice concoction that's heated and thickened, then chilled and folded into whipped cream); the cottage or cream cheese dressings, and the hot dressings used for "Dutch" raw spinach, hot potato salads, and other "hot" salads.

Prepared French dressing, both plain and homogenized, mayonnaise, salad dressing and sour cream are available almost everywhere. In addition, there are many interesting specialty dressings on the market which are adaptable for further variation.

There are also salad dressing mixes. These packaged blends of seasonings are designed to give a specific flavor result to premise-made dressings.

By and large, all salad dressings are easy to make. French dressing is particularly so. It's as simple as combining seasonings, pouring in vinegar and salad oil, then giving the mixture a vigorous shake. The dressing is then ready to use "as is" or to create a series of house-specialty dressings. As a "temporary emulsion" that separates quickly, this dressing requires shaking or beating to re-blend the mixture each time before using.

French dressing is the most versatile dressing. Long preferred as the dressings for green salads, it can be varied infinitely and used with almost any salad. It marinates meat, seafood or poultry for salad making. Similarly, some of the most successful raw or cooked vegetable salads call for marinating in French dressing. As a tip: add it to still-warm cooked potatoes or rice for a quicker, more thorough flavor penetration.

Mayonnaise takes longer to make than French dressing. And there's a little more patience and skill involved. But with a mixer equipped with an oil dispenser, it is neither difficult nor tricky to prepare.

Whether you make your own mayonnaise or rely on a purchased product, store it carefully to maintain it in the best possible condition. Cover tightly to avoid surface evaporation and darkening. Keep refrigerated, away from foods with strong odors, and avoid near-freezing temperatures. Freezing, over-heating, drying of surface, or even sudden jolting, may cause separation.

Mayonnaise is the classic dressing for mixed salads like potato, tuna and chicken. And it is the basis for Russian,

Crisp Greens with Dill Seed Dressing

American Spice Trade Assn.

Thousand Island, Tartar Sauce, and other familiar dressings. As a basic dressing it mingles easily with various seasonings and other additions. Commercial salad dressing combines with other ingredients in much the same way.

Sour cream, a base rather than a finished dressing, also has the potential for a full complement of dressings when the chosen ingredients are folded in. (For variations of basic dressings, see charts on following pages.)

Salad Dressing Variations

DRESSING VARIATION	TO 1 QUART ADD	GOOD WITH . . .
FRENCH DRESSING		
BLUE CHEESE FRENCH DRESSING	¼ pound crumbled Blue cheese	Tossed greens, lettuce wedges, tomato salads, hearts of romaine
VEGETABLE FRENCH DRESSING	1 cup minced celery; 1 cup minced green peppers; 2½ tablespoons minced onion	Tossed greens, tomato salads, green lima bean salad
VINAIGRETTE DRESSING	½ cup minced dill pickles; 3 hard-cooked eggs, minced	Asparagus, green bean and other vegetable salads
EASY ANCHOVY DRESSING	½ cup anchovy paste	Egg salads, mixed greens
CURRY FRENCH DRESSING	¾ teaspoon curry powder; 3 sieved hard-cooked eggs	Greens, shrimp, cooked vegetable salads
BROWN SUGAR-LEMON DRESSING	¾ cup brown sugar; 3 tablespoons lemon juice; 1 tablespoon grated lemon rind	Fresh and canned fruit salads
CELERY SEED DRESSING	½ cup catsup; ¼ cup sugar; 4 teaspoons celery seed; 2 minced garlic cloves	Cooked vegetable salads, shredded Chinese cabbage
CHIFFONADE DRESSING	4 hard-cooked eggs; 4 small beets; 4 small onions, all finely chopped	Slices of lettuce, hearts of romaine, vegetable and tomato salads

Dressing	Ingredients	Uses
NEW ORLEANS DRESSING	1 tablespoon prepared mustard; 1 tablespoon Worcestershire	Vegetable salads, egg salads.
PIQUANT FRENCH DRESSING	2 tablespoons chopped chives; ½ cup mixed relish; ½ cup minced onion; 2 tablespoons chopped tarragon	Egg salads, cooked broccoli, Bibb lettuce, hearts of romaine.
TOMATO DRESSING	1½ cups finely diced fresh tomatoes; 1 teaspoon basil leaves; ½ cup minced onions; 1 teaspoon celery salt.	Mixed greens, shredded lettuce.
HERB FRENCH DRESSING	¼ cup chopped parsley; 2 teaspoons oregano; 1 teaspoon powdered thyme	Greens, egg, vegetable salads.

PREPARED SALAD DRESSING

Dressing	Ingredients	Uses
HONEY CREAM DRESSING	1½ cups honey; fold in 2½ quarts heavy cream, whipped.	Stuffed prune, stuffed apricot, citrus and other fruit salads.
MUSTARD DRESSING	½ cup prepared mustard.	Cold corned beef, tongue. Egg, meat salads. Sandwich spreads.
LEMON DRESSING	¼ cup lemon juice; 2 teaspoons grated lemon rind	Seafood salads, jellied fruit, canned pear salads.
CURRY DRESSING	2 tablespoons curry powder.	Seafood, chicken and egg salads.
PINEAPPLE DRESSING	2 cups drained crushed pineapple.	Canned fruit salads, jellied fruit, cottage cheese.
WHIPPED CREAM DRESSING	1 quart heavy cream, whipped	Fresh, canned and frozen fruit salads. Fruited cabbage slaws.

(cont.)

Salad Dressing Variations (cont.)

DRESSING VARIATION	TO 1 QUART ADD	GOOD WITH . . .
CAVALIER DRESSING	¼ pound crumbled Blue cheese; ¼ cup catsup; 2 tablespoons minced onion; 2 tablespoons vinegar.	Mixed greens, wedges of lettuce.
MAYONNAISE		
GLORIOUS GREENS DRESSING	2 cups Italian dressing; 1 cup shredded Parmesan cheese.	Tossed greens, tomato salads.
HORSERADISH MAYON-NAISE	¼ cup prepared horseradish (let stand several hours).	Cold corned beef, tongue. Tomato aspic, beet, green bean salads.
CUCUMBER MAYON-NAISE	3 cups finely chopped, salted, drained cucumber, salt to taste.	Shrimp, tuna, salmon or egg salads. Tomato aspic.
CHICKEN FLAVOR MAYON-NAISE	1½ to 2 tablespoons chicken soup base.	Chicken or seafood salads, sandwich spreads.
RUSSIAN DRESSING	½ cup sweet pickle relish; 1-1/3 cups chili sauce; 2 cooked eggs, chopped; 1¼ teaspoons salt.	Egg, tomato, asparagus salads, shrimp or crabmeat, green salads, cottage cheese.
DILL MAYONNAISE	¼ cup chopped fresh dill.	Seafood, potato, cooked vegetable, egg and green salads.
CREAMY ROQUEFORT DRESSING	3 cups sour cream; 2¼ cups crumbled Roquefort cheese, loosely packed; salt to taste	Tomato aspic, sliced tomatoes; cooked vegetable salads, pear salad, wedges of lettuce, hearts of romaine.

PINEAPPLE DRESSING	1 cup whipped cream; ¼ cup sugar; 1½ cups drained crushed pineapple	Pear salads, jellied fruit and frozen fruit salads.
RAISIN-NUT DRESSING	1 cup orange juice; ½ cup cut-up raisins; 1 cup chopped nuts	Apple, peach, pear and pineapple salads, Chinese cabbage slaw.
SMITHFIELD DRESSING	1 cup finely chopped Smithfield ham; ¼ cup minced sweet pickles, 2 tablespoons lemon juice; ½ teaspoon celery salt.	Wedges of lettuce, sliced egg, cooked broccoli; green bean, asparagus salads.
SOUR CREAM		
HONEY CREAM DRESSING	Gently stir in 1-1/3 cups honey; 1/8 teaspoon salt. Chill.	Stuffed prune, canned apricot, banana-nut, mixed fruit salads.
PIQUANT COTTAGE CHEESE	2 cups cottage cheese; 1½ teaspoons salt; 1 teaspoon lemon juice; 1/8 teaspoon pepper.	Fruit salads, slices of lettuce, tomato, cucumber salads.
CHILI DRESSING	Mix ¾ cup chili sauce; ¼ cup minced green pepper; ¼ cup minced pimiento; 1 teaspoon salt. Fold into sour cream. Chill.	Shrimp, crabmeat, other fish.
GINGER-NUT CREAM	Mix ½ cup finely cut candied ginger and 1 cup finely chopped walnuts. Fold mixture and 2 tablespoons honey into sour cream.	Pear, pineapple, melon and other fruit salads.

(cont.)

Salad Dressing Variations (cont.)

DRESSING VARIATION	TO 1 QUART ADD	GOOD WITH . . . .
YANKEE DRESSING	Mix 1 cup mayonnaise; ¼ teaspoon salt; 2 teaspoons grated onion. Fold into sour cream. Chill.	Tomato aspic, jellied vegetable, sliced tomato, mixed cooked vegetable, chicken, meat salads.
GOURMET DRESSING	Gently stir in 2/3 cup French dressing; 1 teaspoon salt.	Raw and cooked vegetable, meat and poultry salads.
CHUTNEY DRESSING	1 cup chopped chutney; 2 teaspoons grated lemon rind.	Chicken, turkey; fresh, canned, jellied fruit salads.
CHERRY CREAM DRESSING	Gently stir in ¼ cup chopped maraschino cherries; 1 cup of the cherry juice. Chill.	Pear, grapefruit and other fruit salads.
SWEET AND SOUR DRESSING	Mix 3 tablespoons sugar; 2 teaspoons salt; 2 teaspoons dry mustard; ¼ cup white vinegar. Gently mix into sour cream.	Cooked vegetable salads; slaws, sliced cucumbers.
RED CURRANT CREAM DRESSING	Break up 1½ cups currant jelly with fork. Fold into sour cream.	Fresh and canned fruit salads.

COOKED LEMON SALAD DRESSING

Yield: 1½ quarts

Ingredients

LEMON JUICE, CANNED or FROZEN	1 cup
EGGS	4
SUGAR	½ cup
SALT	2 tablespoons
MUSTARD, DRY	2 tablespoons
SALAD OIL	3 cups
CORNSTARCH	1 cup
WATER	1 quart

Procedure

1. Place lemon juice, unbeaten eggs, seasoning and salad oil in a bowl. Do not stir.

2. Blend cornstarch with 2 cups of water; add remaining water. Cook over low heat, stirring constantly, until mixture thickens and is clear.

3. Add hot cornstarch mixture to ingredients in bowl. Beat quickly with rotary or electric beater until dressing is smooth. Serve with gelatin or fruit salads.

RIPE OLIVE SEAFOOD DRESSING

Yield: 1 gallon

Ingredients

MAYONNAISE	3 cups
SOUR CREAM	3 cups
CHILI SAUCE	1 quart
LEMON JUICE	1 cup
SALT	1 tablespoon
RIPE OLIVES, chopped	3 cups
SHRIMP, cooked	2 pounds (1¼ quarts)

Procedure

1. Blend mayonnaise, sour cream, chili sauce, lemon juice and salt.

2. Add ripe olives and shrimp; mix lightly.

FLUFFY ALMOND FRUIT DRESSING

Yield: 2 quarts

Ingredients

ALMONDS, roasted, diced	1 cup
CELERY, chopped	2 cups
SOUR CREAM	1 quart
MAYONNAISE	2 cups
FROZEN ORANGE JUICE CONCENTRATE	¾ cup (6 ounces)
SUGAR	1 tablespoon
SALT	2 to 3 tablespoons

Procedure
1. Combine all ingredients; chill.
2. Serve over fruit salads.

FRUIT FRENCH DRESSING I

Yield: 1½ quarts

Ingredients

SUGAR	2/3 cup
SALT	1 tablespoon
PAPRIKA	2 teaspoons
SALAD OIL	3 cups
VINEGAR	1 cup
PINEAPPLE JUICE	1 cup
ORANGE JUICE	1 cup

Procedure
1. Combine sugar, salt and paprika. Beat in oil, vinegar, and fruit juices.

SPRINGTIME SALAD DRESSING ⟶

Yield: 1 gallon

Ingredients

MAYONNAISE	2½ quarts
ITALIAN DRESSING	1¼ quarts
BLUE CHEESE, crumbled	13 ounces

3 to 1 BASIC FRENCH DRESSING

Yield: 1 gallon

Ingredients

VEGETABLE OIL	3 quarts
VINEGAR	1 quart
SALT	5 tablespoons
SUGAR	3 tablespoons
PAPRIKA	2 tablespoons
PEPPER	1 tablespoon

Procedure

1. Combine all ingredients, blending with a wire whip. Store in covered container.
2. Shake or beat well before using.

LIME HONEY DRESSING

Yield: 2½ quarts

Ingredients

LIME JUICE	2 cups
HONEY	2 cups
PREPARED MUSTARD	1 tablespoon
SALT	1 tablespoon
LIME RIND, grated	1 tablespoon
SALAD OIL	1½ quarts

Procedure

1. Combine lime juice and honey; blend. Add mustard, salt and grated lime rind.
2. Add salad oil; blend thoroughly. Store in refrigerator.

Procedure

1. Whip mayonnaise, Italian dressing and two-thirds of the cheese until mixture is smooth and emulsified.
2. Stir in remaining blue cheese by hand. Chill.

FRESH ORANGE FRUIT SALAD DRESSING

Yield: 2½ quarts

Ingredients

ORANGE JUICE, FRESH	2 cups
EGG YOLKS	8
LEMON JUICE, FRESH	¼ cup
SALT	½ teaspoon
SUGAR, GRANULATED	1½ cups
EGG WHITES	8
HEAVY CREAM, whipped	1 cup

Procedure

1. Heat orange juice over low heat.
2. Beat egg yolks with fresh lemon juice and salt in top of a double boiler. Gradually beat in half a cup of the sugar.
3. Slowly stir in the hot orange juice; cook over hot, but not boiling water, stirring constantly.
4. Beat egg whites until they stand in soft peaks. Gradually beat in the remaining 1 cup of sugar. Fold into the cooked mixture. Chill.
5. Just before serving, fold in whipped cream.

THOUSAND ISLAND DRESSING

Yield: 1 gallon

Ingredients

ONIONS, grated	1 tablespoon
MUSTARD, PREPARED	2 teaspoons
SWEET PICKLE RELISH	1½ cups
TOMATO SOUP, CONDENSED	1 51-ounce can
MAYONNAISE	1¾ quarts (3½ pounds)
LEMON JUICE	½ cup
EGGS, hard-cooked, chopped	1 quart (10 eggs)

Procedure

1. Combine onion, mustard and relish.
2. Using a whip, blend in soup, then mayonnaise, then lemon juice.
3. Fold in eggs. Chill.

Top with Green Goddess Dressing

American Spice Trade Assn.

FLUFFY RAISIN DRESSING

Yield: approximately 1 quart

Ingredients

RAISINS, LIGHT or DARK	1 cup
SHERRY WINE or ORANGE JUICE	1/4 cup
MAYONNAISE	1 cup
MUSTARD, DRY	1 teaspoon
SALT	1/8 teaspoon
LEMON JUICE	1 tablespoon
MARASCHINO CHERRY SYRUP	1 tablespoon
WHIPPING CREAM	1 cup

Procedure

1. Rinse and drain raisins thoroughly. Chop coarsely; add wine or orange juice. Let stand several hours or overnight.

2. Blend mayonnaise, mustard, salt, lemon juice and cherry syrup. Add raisins.

3. Whip cream stiff; fold into mayonnaise mixture.

SWEET-SOUR DRESSING

Yield: 2¼ quarts

Ingredients

SUGAR	1½ cups
SALT	3 tablespoons
MUSTARD, DRY	2 tablespoons
CORNSTARCH	1 tablespoon
PEPPER, WHITE, GROUND	¼ teaspoon
CAYENNE	dash
VINEGAR	3 cups
SALAD OIL	1½ quarts

Procedure

1. Combine dry ingredients in a tall kettle with tight-fitting lid. (Use tall kettle to avoid boiling over.)

2. Add vinegar; heat, stirring occasionally, until mixture boils. Cover; reduce heat. Boil exactly 5 minutes. Cool.

3. Add salad oil slowly, beating with a whip.

Note

Dressing separates on standing. Before using, beat to mix thoroughly.

POPPY SEED DRESSING

Yield: 9 gallons

Ingredients

SUGAR	4 gallons
MUSTARD, DRY	2 cups
VINEGAR, CIDER	2 gallons
SALAD OIL	4 gallons
POPPY SEED	1 quart
ONIONS, grated	1 quart
SALT	½ cup

Procedure

1. Combine sugar and dry mustard; mix. Add vinegar; stir to dissolve. Bring to a boil, boil one minute.

2. Let mixture cool.

3. Beat in oil, adding slowly. Add poppy seed, onion and salt.

RIPE OLIVE THOUSAND ISLAND DRESSING

Yield: approximately 3¾ quarts

Ingredients

ONIONS, CHOPPED, DRIED	2 tablespoons
WATER	2 tablespoons
MAYONNAISE	1-1/2 quarts
CATSUP	3 cups
PICKLES, chopped	1-1/2 cups
RIPE OLIVES, chopped	3 cups
EGGS, hard-cooked, chopped	3
WORCESTERSHIRE SAUCE	1 tablespoon
VINEGAR	1/3 cup
HOT PEPPER SAUCE	1/4 teaspoon

Procedure

1. Combine onions with water; let stand 5 to 10 minutes.
2. Blend all ingredients together thoroughly.

COTTAGE CHEESE FRENCH DRESSING

Yield: 2½ quarts

Ingredients

COTTAGE CHEESE	1 quart
SUGAR	½ cup
SALT	2 tablespoons
MUSTARD, DRY	3 tablespoons
PAPRIKA	1½ tablespoons
GARLIC POWDER	1 tablespoon
VINEGAR	2 cups
SALAD OIL	1 quart
CATSUP	1 cup
ONION, grated	½ cup
HOT PEPPER SAUCE	¼ teaspoon

Procedure.

1. Whip cheese until creamy.
2. Mix sugar, salt, mustard, paprika and garlic powder. Blend with vinegar. Add to cottage cheese.
3. Add remaining ingredients; beat until well blended.

VINAIGRETTE DRESSING

Yield: approximately 2 quarts

Ingredients

MUSTARD, POWDERED	2 tablespoons
WATER, warm	2 tablespoons
SALT	¼ cup
SUGAR	2 tablespoons
MONOSODIUM GLUTAMATE	1 tablespoon
PEPPER, BLACK, GROUND	2 teaspoons
GARLIC, finely minced	2 teaspoons
ONION, finely minced	½ cup
PARSLEY, chopped	½ cup
TARRAGON LEAVES	¼ cup
VINEGAR	1½ cups
LEMON JUICE, FRESH	½ cup
SALAD OIL	1½ quarts

Procedure

1. Blend mustard with water. Let stand 10 minutes to develop flavor.
2. Add remaining seasonings, vinegar and lemon juice; mix well.
3. Add oil; mix thoroughly.
4. Refrigerate at least 2 hours before serving.

AVOCADO MAYONNAISE

Yield: approximately 1-1/8 gallons

Ingredients

MUSTARD	1 tablespoon
SALT	2 to 3 teaspoons
VINEGAR, TARRAGON	¼ cup
LEMON JUICE from	2 lemons
ONION, grated	1
MAYONNAISE	1 gallon
AVOCADOS, mashed	6

Procedure

1. Combine mustard, salt, vinegar, lemon juice and grated onion. Add to mayonnaise; blend thoroughly. Fold in mashed avocados.

MAYONNAISE PIQUANT

Yield: 1¼ quarts

Ingredients

MAYONNAISE	1 quart
LEMON JUICE	½ cup
MUSTARD, PREPARED	3 to 4 tablespoons
HORSERADISH	3 to 4 tablespoons
WORCESTERSHIRE SAUCE	1 tablespoon
HOT PEPPER SAUCE	½ teaspoon
INSTANT MINCED ONION	1 teaspoon
PARSLEY, chopped	¾ cup

Procedure

1. Combine ingredients; chill. Serve with tomato aspic.

TOMATO FRENCH DRESSING
(using tomato soup)

Yield: 1 gallon

Ingredients

SUGAR	3/4 cup
SALT	2 tablespoons
MUSTARD, DRY	2 tablespoons
PAPRIKA	2 teaspoons
PEPPER, WHITE	1 teaspoon
ONION, finely chopped	2/3 cup (4 ounces)
TOMATO SOUP, CONDENSED	1 51-ounce can
VINEGAR, CIDER	3 cups
OIL, SALAD	1-1/2 quarts

Procedure

1. Mix dry ingredients; blend in onion, soup and vinegar.
2. Add oil gradually, blending in with a wire whip. Mix well before serving.

Variations

1. Add 4 teaspoons curry powder.
2. Add 4 teaspoons Italian seasoning.
3. Add 2 tablespoons crushed tarragon leaves.
4. Blend in 8 ounces mashed blue cheese.

CREAMY ROQUEFORT SALAD DRESSING

Yield: 1¼ quarts

Ingredients

CHEESE, ROQUEFORT	6 ounces
SOUR CREAM	1 quart
VINEGAR, CIDER	2 tablespoons
SALT	1 tablespoon
PEPPER, GROUND	½ teaspoon
PARSLEY, chopped	3 tablespoons
ONION, grated	2 teaspoons

Procedure

1. Have Roquefort cheese at room temperature for 1 to 1½ hours for easy mixing. Cream the cheese thoroughly. Add sour cream gradually, mixing well with a wire whip.

2. Add vinegar, salt, pepper, parsley and onion; mix thoroughly. Refrigerate until serving time.

3. Serve with mixed green salad, hearts of lettuce or romaine.

Note

Salad dressing can be refrigerated for 7 to 10 days.

FRUIT FRENCH DRESSING II

Yield: 1¼ quarts

Ingredients

LEMON JUICE	1 cup
ORANGE JUICE	½ cup
SALAD OIL	3 cups
SUGAR	¼ cup
SALT	4 teaspoons
PEPPER, WHITE	¼ teaspoon
CURRANT JELLY (optional)	1 cup

Procedure

1. Combine fruit juices, salad oil and seasonings in a bowl; beat with wire whip.

2. Soften jelly with whip; beat into the mixture. (For best flavor, use dressing the same day it is prepared.) Serve with fresh fruit or jellied fruit salads.

GREEN GODDESS DRESSING

Yield: approximately 2 quarts

Ingredients

MAYONNAISE	1 quart
SOUR CREAM	2½ cups
ANCHOVY PASTE	½ cup
VINEGAR, TARRAGON-WINE	¾ cup
WORCESTERSHIRE SAUCE	1 tablespoon
CHIVES or SCALLIONS, chopped	¾ cup
PARSLEY, chopped	1 cup
GARLIC	3 cloves
MUSTARD, DRY	2 teaspoons
SALT	2 teaspoons
PEPPER, BLACK	½ teaspoon

Procedure

1. Combine mayonnaise, sour cream, anchovy paste, vinegar, Worcestershire sauce, chives and parsley.

2. Crush garlic with mustard, salt and pepper. Add to mayonnaise mixture, blending thoroughly.

TRIM LINE COTTAGE CHEESE SALAD DRESSING

Yield: approximately 2 quarts

Ingredients

COTTAGE CHEESE	2½ pounds
BUTTERMILK	2 cups
HARD-COOKED EGGS, sieved	8
GREEN PEPPER, minced	1 cup
RADISHES, minced	1 cup
LEMON JUICE	¼ cup
SALT	2 teaspoons
PAPRIKA	2 teaspoons
INSTANT GRANULATED GARLIC	1 teaspoon

Procedure

1. Combine all ingredients; beat on mixer until blended and creamy. Chill.

2. Shake or mix well before serving.

Creamy Dressing for Lettuce Wedges

Western Iceberg Lettuce, Inc.

COOKED PAPRIKA SOUR CREAM DRESSING

Yield: 1 quart

Ingredients

POWDERED MUSTARD	4 teaspoons
WATER	4 teaspoons
SALT	1 tablespoon
SUGAR	3 tablespoons
FLOUR	3 tablespoons
PAPRIKA	1 tablespoon
CAYENNE	¼ teaspoon
EGG YOLKS, beaten	5
VINEGAR	¾ cup
BUTTER or MARGARINE, melted	¼ cup
SOUR CREAM	2½ cups

Procedure

1. Combine mustard and water; let stand 10 minutes for flavor to develop.

2. Combine salt, sugar, flour, paprika and cayenne; stir in mustard. Beat in egg yolks and vinegar.

3. Cook and stir mixture over hot water until smooth and thick. Blend in butter. Cool.

4. Fold in sour cream.

Serve with meats, seafood, poultry, egg or vegetable salads.

FLORIDA LOW-CALORIE FRENCH DRESSING

Yield: 1 gallon

Ingredients

GRAPEFRUIT JUICE, CANNED, UNSWEETENED	3 quarts
CORNSTARCH	½ cup
SALAD OIL	1½ cups
SALT	2½ tablespoons
SUGAR	6 tablespoons
PAPRIKA	1 tablespoon
MUSTARD, DRY	1 tablespoon
HOT PEPPER SAUCE	1 tablespoon
CATSUP	3 cups
GARLIC (optional)	4 cloves

Procedure

1. Blend 3 cups of the grapefruit juice with cornstarch. Cook and stir over low heat until thickened. Remove from heat; stir in remaining grapefruit juice.

2. Combine oil with remaining ingredients except garlic. Add grapefruit mixture; beat until blended.

3. Add garlic, if desired. Store, covered, in refrigerator.

4. Shake or stir before serving.

TOMATO CHEESE DRESSING (Low Calorie)

Yield: 1¼ quarts

Ingredients

GARLIC, peeled	3 cloves
SALT	1½ teaspoons
TOMATO SOUP, CONDENSED	1 quart
WINE VINEGAR	1/3 cup
COTTAGE CHEESE	1 pound

Procedure

1. Mash garlic in salt until finely ground.

2. Add remaining ingredients; mix well. Chill.

3. Serve with lettuce or other salad greens or with drained, chilled cooked or canned vegetables.

EGGLESS MAYONNAISE

Yield: 1½ gallons

Ingredients

SUGAR	½ cup
PAPRIKA	1 tablespoon
SALT	¼ cup
PEPPER	1 teaspoon
DRY MUSTARD	2 tablespoons
EVAPORATED MILK, undiluted	1½ quarts
SALAD OIL	1 gallon
VINEGAR	2 cups

Procedure

1. Combine dry ingredients in mixer bowl. Add evaporated milk; mix well with spoon.

2. Beat at medium speed. Add 3 quarts of the salad oil slowly allowing 5 minutes for each quart of oil added.

3. Add vinegar very slowly alternating with remaining oil.

4. Chill well before serving. (Mayonnaise thickens when chilled. Thin with evaporated milk, if desired.)

TWO-CHEESE SALAD DRESSING

Yield: 1 gallon

Ingredients

BLUE CHEESE, crumbled	2 pounds
CREAM CHEESE, softened	2½ pounds
MAYONNAISE	1¼ quarts
MILK	1¼ cups
SUGAR	1 tablespoon
LEMON JUICE	2 tablespoons
BLUE CHEESE, crumbled	½ pound

Procedure

1. Combine first amount of blue cheese, cream cheese, mayonnaise, milk and sugar in mixer bowl. Beat to blend.

2. Add lemon juice; blend.

3. Stir in remaining blue cheese by hand.

4. Serve with fruit or sliced tomato salads.

LOUIS DRESSING

Yield: 2 quarts

Ingredients

CREAM, HEAVY (for whipping)	1 cup
MAYONNAISE	1 quart
LEMON RIND, grated	1 tablespoon
LEMON JUICE	1/3 cup
CHILI SAUCE	2-1/2 cups
GREEN PEPPER, chopped	1 cup
CELERY, chopped	1 cup
SALT	1 tablespoon
PEPPER	1/8 teaspoon
ONION, finely chopped	3 tablespoons

Procedure
1. Whip cream.
2. Combine mayonnaise with remaining ingredients.
3. Fold in whipped cream, blending well. Chill.

ITALIAN DRESSING

Yield: approximately 3½ quarts

Ingredients

EGG YOLKS	4
PEPPER, BLACK, COARSE GRIND	2 tablespoons
SALT	2 tablespoons
GARLIC, minced	2 cloves
MUSTARD, DRY	2 teaspoons
LEMON JUICE from	3 lemons
WORCESTERSHIRE SAUCE	1 tablespoon
ANCHOVY FILLETS	10
WINE VINEGAR	1½ cups
SALAD OIL	3 quarts

Procedure
1. Combine egg yolks, seasonings, lemon juice, Worcestershire sauce, anchovy fillets and wine vinegar in blender. Blend thoroughly.
2. Add 3 quarts oil; blend for 30 seconds.

MAYONNAISE

Yield: approximately 6 gallons

Ingredients

EGGS, whole	3 pounds, 12 ounces
SALT	8½ ounces
SUGAR	7½ ounces
MUSTARD, DRY	3 ounces
SALAD OIL	5 gallons
VINEGAR, CIDER, 50-GRAIN	1¾ quarts

Procedure

1. Have eggs, oil and vinegar cold (50° to 55°F.) if possible.
2. Beat eggs at high speed of mixer 2 minutes.
3. Mix salt, sugar and mustard. Add to beaten eggs; beat 2 minutes.
4. Add oil in fine stream while continuing to beat at high speed. Gradually increase flow of oil as emulsion builds up. Add all of oil in 10 to 15 minutes.
5. Add small amounts of vinegar if necessary during addition of oil to keep emulsion from breaking. Add remainder after oil is in, with mixer running at lower speed.
6. Scrape down bowl; beat for an additional minute to finish batch.

VARIATIONS

PARTY DRESSING

MAYONNAISE	2 quarts
STUFFED OLIVES, chopped	1 cup
COTTAGE CHEESE, COARSE TYPE	2 cups

Procedure

1. Blend to a uniform mixture. (Better if aged 2 days before use.)

ROQUEFORT DRESSING ⟶

ROQUEFORT CHEESE	1 pound
MAYONNAISE	2 quarts
CHILI SAUCE	2 cups
PAPRIKA	1 ounce

COLE SLAW DRESSING

Yield: 5½ quarts

Ingredients

MAYONNAISE	1 gallon
PREPARED MUSTARD	1 cup
VINEGAR, CIDER	2 cups
LEMON JUICE	1 cup
VINEGAR, WINE	1 cup
SUGAR	2 cups
SALT	as needed
PEPPER	as needed

Procedure
1. Combine ingredients, adding salt and pepper to taste.
2. Refrigerate to blend flavors.

FRESH ORANGE CREAM CHEESE SALAD DRESSING

Yield: approximately 2 quarts

Ingredients

CREAM CHEESE	3 pounds
ORANGE JUICE, fresh	1 quart
SALT	1/2 teaspoon
SUGAR	1/3 cup

Procedure
1. Soften cream cheese; combine with remaining ingredients.
2. Serve over fresh fruit salads.

Procedure
1. Run cold Roquefort cheese through ¼-inch shredder into a small amount of cornstarch. Sprinkle lightly with the cornstarch and toss gently to break shreds into short pieces.
2. Combine cheese with other ingredients blending carefully to a uniform mixture.

A Choice of Special Dressings

Western Iceberg Lettuce, Inc.

RANDALL HOUSE DRESSING

Yield: 3½ quarts

Ingredients

EVAPORATED MILK	2½ quarts
VINEGAR	3 cups
ONION SOUP MIX, DEHYDRATED	9 ounces
CATSUP	2 cups
WORCESTERSHIRE SAUCE	1 tablespoon
HOT PEPPER SAUCE	1 teaspoon

Procedure

1. Combine evaporated milk and vinegar.

2. Add remaining ingredients. Blend thoroughly, using a wire whip. Chill. Serve over mixed green, vegetable or seafood salads, or toss with cabbage for cole slaw.

FRENCH BLUE CHEESE DRESSING

Yield: approximately 2¼ gallons

Ingredients

SALAD OIL	1 gallon
ONION, grated	½ cup
CELERY SALT	6 tablespoons
PAPRIKA	¾ cup
WORCESTERSHIRE SAUCE	1 cup
CATSUP	2 quarts
SUGAR	1 cup
WATER	1 cup
LEMON JUICE, FRESH	1½ quarts
VINEGAR	2 cups
GARLIC, crushed	4 cloves
BLUE CHEESE, crumbled	½ pound

Procedure

1. Mix oil, onion, celery salt, paprika, Worcestershire sauce and catsup.
2. Dissolve sugar in water; boil until it spins a thread (to 230°F.).
3. Add syrup, lemon juice, vinegar and garlic to oil mixture; blend well. Chill.
4. Add crumbled blue cheese to chilled mixture.

ONION FRENCH DRESSING

Yield: 1 gallon

Ingredients

SALAD OIL	2-1/2 quarts
WINE VINEGAR	1-1/4 quarts
INSTANT MINCED ONION	2 ounces (2/3 cup)
SALT	3 tablespoons
DRY MUSTARD	3 tablespoons
PAPRIKA	1 tablespoon
DILL, dried	2 teaspoons
HOT PEPPER SAUCE	1/2 teaspoon
SOY SAUCE	1/3 cup

Procedure

1. Combine ingredients; beat until blended.

FRUIT SALAD DRESSING ⟶

Yield: 1 gallon

Ingredients

ORANGE JUICE	3 cups
PINEAPPLE JUICE	3 cups
LEMON JUICE	½ cup
CORNSTARCH, MODIFIED	5 tablespoons
SUGAR	6 tablespoons
SALT	1 teaspoon
EGGS, beaten	8
WHIPPING CREAM, whipped	1 quart

PIQUANT SALAD DRESSING FOR FRUIT

Yield: 3½ quarts

Ingredients

SUGAR	10 ounces
SALT	2 tablespoons
MUSTARD, DRY	1 tablespoon
PAPRIKA	¼ cup
CELERY SEED	3 tablespoons
LEMON JUICE, FRESH	1 quart
LIME JUICE, FRESH	2 cups
HONEY	1 pound
SALAD OIL	1½ quarts

Procedure

1. Mix sugar, salt, mustard, paprika and celery seed.
2. Add lemon and lime juice; blend in honey.
3. Add salad oil, mixing well.
4. Shake or mix well before using.

Procedure

1. Heat the fruit juices to boiling. Mix cornstarch, sugar and salt; add to the hot mixture. Cook and stir until thickened.

2. Add a small amount of the hot mixture to the beaten eggs; add to remainder of hot mixture. Cook for a few minutes. Remove from heat. Cool.

3. Fold the whipped cream into the cold mixture. Refrigerate.

Iceberg Raft with Cottage Cheese Dressing (See recipe, p. 225)

Western Iceberg Lettuce, Inc.

Iceberg Lettuce and Topping

MANY people consider a salad the perfect luncheon regardless of the weather. But on too-warm-for-comfort days, the well made green salad that packs a hearty extra can triple its appeal.

A brand new concept of this proven favorite—topped iceberg salad—is less work than a chef's salad and a refreshing change. It offers a number of welcome advantages to help improve production in a busy salad room.

The principle of these salads is simple. They are comprised of cold, thoroughly crisp iceberg lettuce cut in a slice or "raft" and generously covered with a rich, flavorful, thicker-than-dressing topping. The shape of the lettuce is important. It is a flat-lying slice cut straight across the head, not a wedge. And for heartiness and satiety value, it is essential that the topping contain a fair amount of a substantial, protein-rich food such as cheese, chicken, seafood or egg. It should have enough "body" to mound a little, or at least to stay in place on the lettuce and not run off.

You can base the toppings on mayonnaise, cottage cheese or sour cream. As an example, add shrimp and/or crab meat to mayonnaise, well seasoned with catsup and horseradish, for *a seafood version (this one, a simplified Louis dressing). You can make a whole series of interesting toppings starting out with the well-known sour cream and dried onion soup mixture that's popularly known as California Dip. Avoid combinations that make overly-rich mixtures; the salad shouldn't become cloying to the palate before it is all consumed.*

Both topping and "green" can be prepared ahead. When making a sizeable number of salads, you can slice the lettuce and arrange on bun pans to cover and stack. Assembling the salad is quick and easy. Simply set the slice of lettuce onto crisp greens or in an open lettuce cup. Spoon on the topping or portion with a scoop and add something in the way of a garnish to give an accent of color or a texture contrast.

*The charm of this salad lies in its simplicity, its good eating qualities and manageability on the plate. Choose the garnish carefully and arrange it tastefully—avoid any appearance of fussiness. Overdecoration here (as elsewhere) is **not** the smart touch!*

LETTUCE WITH GENOA TOPPING

Yield: 24 portions

Ingredients

SALAMI, finely ground	1 pound
SOUR CREAM	2 cups
MAYONNAISE	½ cup
GREEN ONIONS, finely chopped	2/3 cup
CHILI SAUCE	½ cup
SALT	1 teaspoon
ICEBERG LETTUCE, ¾-inch slices	24
SALAD GREENS	as needed

Procedure

1. Combine salami, sour cream, mayonnaise, green onions, chili sauce and salt. Chill.

2. Arrange lettuce slices on salad greens. Top with dressing allowing 1½ ounces per salad.

LETTUCE WITH COUNTRY GARDEN TOPPING

Yield: 25 portions

Ingredients

CUCUMBERS, peeled, halved, sliced	1 quart
GREEN ONIONS, thinly sliced	1-1/3 cups
SOUR CREAM	1 quart
WINE VINEGAR	1-1/2 tablespoons
SALT	4 teaspoons
WHITE PEPPER	1/2 teaspoon
PARSLEY, FRESH, chopped	1 cup
CHEESE, SHARP CHEDDAR, shredded	1 pound
ICEBERG LETTUCE, 3/4-inch crosswise slices	25
SALAD GREENS	as needed

Procedure

1. Peel cucumbers. Cut into halves lengthwise; remove large seeds, if necessary. Slice.

2. Slice green onions (include tender portions of top).

3. Combine sour cream, vinegar, salt and pepper. Add cucumbers, onions, and parsley. Fold in cheese. Refrigerate 20 minutes or more to blend flavors.

4. Arrange lettuce slices on greens. Top with a No. 12 scoop of the cucumber mixture, spreading over surface of lettuce slice. Sprinkle with paprika and additional chopped parsley, if desired.

SEAFOOD TOPPING

Yield: 3 quarts

Ingredients

MAYONNAISE	1½ quarts
LEMON JUICE	2 tablespoons
HORSERADISH	¼ cup
CATSUP	¾ cup
SALT	1 tablespoon
CRABMEAT or SHRIMP, cooked, split (or a mixture of both)	1¼ quarts
AVOCADO, diced*	3 cups

Procedure

1. Combine mayonnaise, lemon juice, horseradish, catsup and salt; mix well.

2. Fold in seafood and avocado.

3. Serve on slices of iceberg lettuce. Garnish with whole shrimp and slices of avocado, if desired.

*For an all-seafood version, omit avocado and substitute an equal amount of crabmeat, shrimp or lobster.

AVOCADO CHEESE TOPPING

Yield: 2 quarts

Ingredients

AVOCADO, diced	1 quart
LEMON JUICE	½ cup
COTTAGE CHEESE	1 pound
SOUR CREAM	2½ cups
SALT	2 teaspoons
HOT PEPPER SAUCE	¼ teaspoon
PIMIENTOES, chopped	3 tablespoons

Procedure

1. Mix diced avocado with lemon juice.

2. Add remaining ingredients; mix lightly. Chill.

3. Serve on slices of iceberg lettuce. Garnish with ripe olives and carrot curls, if desired.

CALIFORNIA DIP

Yield: approximately 2 quarts

Ingredients

ONION SOUP MIX	1 6-ounce can
SOUR CREAM	2 quarts

Procedure

1. Thoroughly blend soup mix into sour cream.
2. Cover; refrigerate 1 hour before using.

CALIFORNIA GREEN GODDESS TOPPING

Yield: approximately 2½ quarts

Ingredients

CALIFORNIA DIP	2 quarts
EGGS, hard-cooked, coarsely chopped	8 (3 cups)
ANCHOVY FILLETS, drained, coarsely chopped	¼ cup

Procedure

1. Combine California dip with eggs and anchovies.
2. Cover; refrigerate at least 1 hour before using.
3. Serve on slices of iceberg lettuce. Garnish with anchovy fillet and sieved egg yolk or, with chopped parsley, sliced egg and a tomato wedge.

CREAMY DILLY CRABMEAT TOPPING

Yield: 3¼ quarts

Ingredients

CALIFORNIA DIP	2 quarts
CRABMEAT, drained, flaked	3 15-ounce cans
DILL, fresh, chopped	2 tablespoons
or DRIED DILL WEED	1 teaspoon

Procedure

1. Combine California dip, crabmeat and dill. Cover; refrigerate at least 1 hour before using.
2. Serve on slices of iceberg lettuce. Garnish with radish roses and cress, if desired.

SPRINGTIME VEGETABLE TOPPING

Yield: 3¾ quarts

Ingredients

CALIFORNIA DIP	2 quarts
COTTAGE CHEESE, CREAMED	1 quart
CUCUMBER, finely chopped	2 cups
GREEN PEPPER, finely chopped	1 cup
RADISHES, coarsely chopped	1 cup

Procedure

1. Combine California dip with cottage cheese, cucumber, green pepper and radishes.

2. Cover; refrigerate at least 1 hour before using.

3. Serve on slices of iceberg lettuce. Garnish with a green pepper ring and a radish rose or with tomato wedges and watercress.

CURRIED CHICKEN TOPPING

Yield: 1 quart

Ingredients

CHICKEN, cooked, diced	1½ cups
MAYONNAISE	1½ cups
SOUR CREAM	1 cup
LEMON JUICE	3 tablespoons
CURRY POWDER	1½ tablespoons

Procedure

1. Combine ingredients; mix well. Chill.

2. Serve on slices of iceberg lettuce. Garnish with cherry tomatoes and sprigs of parsley, if desired.

ICEBERG RAFT WITH COTTAGE CHEESE DRESSING

Yield: 24 portions   *(See picture, p. 218)*

Ingredients

WESTERN ICEBERG LETTUCE	about 9 pounds
	(6 heads)
MAYONNAISE	1½ cups
ONION, grated	1 tablespoon
LEMON JUICE	1 tablespoon
SALT	1½ teaspoons
WHITE PEPPER	¼ teaspoon
SOUR CREAM	1½ cups
COTTAGE CHEESE, creamed	3 pounds

Procedure

1. Trim, core, rinse and drain lettuce. Chill well to crisp.

2. Combine mayonnaise, onion, lemon juice, salt and pepper. Fold in sour cream and cottage cheese.

3. Remove large lettuce leaves for "cups." Cut remainder of head crosswise into "rafts."

4. To prepare each salad: Line serving plate with lettuce cup and top with raft. Portion cottage cheese mixture with No. 12 scoop and spread over surface of raft. Sprinkle with paprika. Garnish with watercress, if desired.

NUTTY BLUE CHEESE TOPPING

Yield: 2¾ quarts

Ingredients

CALIFORNIA DIP	2 quarts
BLUE CHEESE, crumbled	1 pound
WALNUTS, finely chopped	8 ounces (2 cups)

Procedure

1. Combine California dip with blue cheese and walnuts.

2. Cover; refrigerate at least 1 hour before using.

3. Serve on slices of iceberg lettuce. Garnish with walnut half and thin apple slices, if desired.

Salad Bar at Don Roth's on Pearson

Mexican stoneware jars on salad bar are part of the decor at Don Roth's on Pearson, Chicago; hold 4 dressing choices (names of dressing on brass plates behind jars); 5th jar holds thin-sliced red onions or herbed croutons. Large salad bowl holds ½ crate crisp-chilled chopped lettuce. Oblong salad dishes at head of line are chilled to keep lettuce at optimal eating temperature. Small brown souffle dishes hold bacon flavored bits, chopped hard-cooked egg, marinated garbanzos, grated parmesan, shredded cheddar cheese while old coffee grinder dispenses cracked pepper. Proof of the popularity of the salad bar is the daily luncheon demand for 2 bowls (1 crate of lettuce) and a Saturday night record of 2 or 3 crates of lettuce.

SALAD BAR
OR BUFFET

ONE of the most colorful parts of the menu, salads make excellent material for an exciting display as a salad bar or buffet.

There's a wide variety of salads that are well suited for
this plan, as well as a full assortment of dressings, appetizing
toppings and other tasty additions. All told, the salad buffet
is a flexible scheme, loaded with potential for original plan-
ning.

As an accessory to the luncheon or dinner meal, you can
base your buffet on a single salad or offer a selection that includes a number of kinds. At noontime you can go further
and offer a buffet of hearty, satisfying salads that are the
mainstay of the meal.

The focal point of a one-salad feature could well be an
ample-sized bowl of mixed salad greens, deliciously chilled.
Or, wedges of brittle-crisp iceberg lettuce piled high in a bowl.
You can weave bits of color through the salad greens by select-
ing one or more of the **salad bowl additions** listed on page 7.
Or, you can offer these frills by arranging them nearby in separate bowls, along with a selection of dressings that invite
patrons to combine salads to their own taste. (See picture,
facing page.)

As another approach, you can map out a plan for a

Small Salad Buffet

American Dairy Assn.

This easily arranged, small, do-it-yourself salad set up offers small bowls of these toppings: (l to r) croutons; cherry tomatoes; cubed cheddar cheese and julienne swiss; hard-cooked egg triangles; julienne tongue or corned beef; crumbled blue cheese.

several-salad buffet, and vary it endlessly within the framework of a general outline. You could, for example, use these as a pattern: a vegetable salad, a gelatin mold, a hearty salad, and either a fruit salad or a relish tray

The vegetable salad can take the form of a cooked vegetable combination that's already mixed. Or, of a selection of appropriate vegetables, cooked just to the crisp-tender stage and arranged in an eye-catching display that bids patrons to express their creative talents. (Salad greens and dressings should be near at hand.) Slaws, pickled beets, marinated tomato slices, 3-bean salad, and cucumbers in sour cream are

Tableside Salad Service

American Dairy Assn.

Toppings for this Imperial Salad Bowl are wheeled alongside table where they are added as salad is served. Salad completes luncheon menu of Petite Cheddar Burgers and milk. Servings from a salad bowl or buffet are being offered more frequently as a sandwich accompaniment.

among other likely candidates for the vegetable spot.

Tomato aspic joins the various jellied vegetable and fruit salads with popular appeal. And, chicken salads, tuna-stuffed avocado halves and ripe tomatoes filled with egg salad or cottage cheese illustrate salads in the substantial class. The makings for fruit salad, as a suggestion, could be one of these: sliced oranges, a Waldorf salad, stuffed peach or pear halves, or simply a bowlful of fresh and canned fruit, cut in attractive large pieces.

Whatever the plan for patron-created salads, they are high on the list of popular dining-out experiences.

A BONUS OF
MOLDED SALADS

Green Giant Co.

Pictured at left and above are (across top) Sunshine Relish Mold, Petits Pois 'N Pickle Mold, (center) Green Garden Mold, (bottom) Tomato Flame Mold. Recipes for these salads appear on the following pages together with several additional molded salad specialties.

SUNSHINE RELISH MOLD

Yield: 48 portions   *(See picture, top, p. 230)*

Ingredients

GELATIN, LEMON	1½ pounds
SALT	4 teaspoons
TURMERIC	1 teaspoon
WATER, boiling	2 quarts
WATER, cold	1½ quarts
WHOLE KERNEL CORN WITH SWEET PEPPERS, drained	½ 75-ounce can (No. 10 vacuum pack can)
SWEET PICKLE RELISH	1 quart

Procedure

1. Dissolve gelatin, salt and turmeric in boiling water.
2. Add cold water; chill until slightly thickened.
3. Fold in remaining ingredients. Turn into individual molds or 12-inch by 20-inch pan. Chill until firm.
4. Unmold or cut into squares. Serve on crisp salad greens.

PETITS POIS 'N PICKLE MOLD
(See picture, top, p. 231)

Yield: 48 portions

Ingredients

BEEF BOUILLON CUBES	18
WATER, boiling	2 quarts
GELATIN, LEMON	1-1/2 pounds
WORCESTERSHIRE SAUCE	1/3 cup
WATER, cold	1-1/2 quarts
PEAS, small, drained	1/2 No. 10 can
CHEESE, AMERICAN, diced	2 cups
DILL PICKLE, diced	2 cups

Procedure

1. Add bouillon cubes to boiling water; heat and stir until dissolved. Pour over gelatin; stir until gelatin is dissolved.

2. Add Worcestershire sauce and cold water. Chill until slightly thickened.

3. Fold in remaining ingredients. Turn into individual molds or 12-inch by 20-inch pan. Chill until firm.

4. Unmold or cut into squares. Serve on crisp salad greens.

TOMATO FLAME MOLD

Yield: 48 portions *(See picture, p. 230, lower left)*

Ingredients

GELATIN, ORANGE	1½ pounds
WATER, boiling	2 quarts
VINEGAR, WINE	¾ cup
ONION JUICE	4 teaspoons
WATER, cold	1½ quarts
PEAS, drained	½ No. 10 can
CUCUMBER, diced	3 cups
CHERRY TOMATOES, small, halved	12 ounces
	(24 whole)

Procedure

1. Dissolve gelatin in boiling water.

2. Add vinegar, onion juice and cold water. Chill until slightly thickened.

3. Fold in remaining ingredients. Turn into individual molds or 12-inch by 20-inch pan. Chill until firm.

4. Unmold or cut into squares. Serve on crisp salad greens.

GREEN GARDEN MOLD

(See picture, p. 231, center)

Yield: 48 portions

Ingredients

GELATIN, LIME	1-1/2 pounds
SALT	4 teaspoons
WATER, boiling	2 quarts
VINEGAR, TARRAGON	1/3 cup
WATER, cold	1-1/2 quarts
GREEN BEANS, diagonal-cut, drained	1/2 No. 10 can
CAULIFLOWER, sliced	3 cups
PIMIENTOES, diced	1 7-ounce can
ONION, finely chopped	1/4 cup

Procedure

1. Dissolve gelatin and salt in boiling water.

2. Add vinegar and cold water. Chill until slightly thickened.

3. Fold in remaining ingredients. Turn into individual molds or 12-inch by 20-inch pan. Chill until firm.

4. Unmold or cut into squares. Serve on crisp salad greens.

ALOHA COTTAGE CHEESE SALAD

Yield: 54 portions

Ingredients

CREAMED COTTAGE CHEESE	9 pounds
SOUR CREAM	1-1/2 cups
GREEN PEPPER, diced	2 cups
PINEAPPLE, crushed (packed in juice, not syrup)	3 cups
CELERY, PASCAL, diced	1-1/2 cups
SALT	1 tablespoon
WATER	1-1/2 cups
LEMON JUICE	1/3 cup
PINEAPPLE JUICE, unsweetened	1 cup
GELATIN, LEMON	10 ounces
GOLDEN DRESSING*	1-3/4 quarts

Procedure

1. Combine cottage cheese, sour cream, green pepper, pineapple, celery and salt; mix lightly but thoroughly. Chill.

2. Combine water, lemon juice, pineapple juice and gelatin. Place over low heat; stir until dissolved. Cool to room temperature.

3. Add cooled gelatin to chilled cheese mixture; mix well.

4. Pour into shallow pans or individual molds. Chill until firm.

5. Serve with Golden Dressing; garnish with additional green pepper and pineapple, if desired.

Note

Salad may be used as part of a cold plate with cold cuts, potato chips and date nut bread.

*GOLDEN DRESSING

Yield: 1¾ quarts

Ingredients

HONEY	1½ cups
SOUR CREAM	1½ quarts

Procedure

Gently blend honey into sour cream. Chill.

THANKSGIVING SALAD

Yield: 25 portions

Ingredients

GELATIN, ORANGE	6 ounces
WATER, boiling	2 cups
WATER, cold	2 cups
CRUSHED PINEAPPLE	12 ounces
PRUNES, chopped	4 ounces
CELERY, finely chopped	4 ounces
NUTS, finely chopped	2 ounces
MARSHMALLOWS, miniature	2 ounces
CHERRIES, MARASCHINO, finely sliced	8
CREAM MAYONNAISE	1½ cups

Procedure

1. Dissolve gelatin in boiling water. Add cold water and crushed pineapple. Chill until slightly thickened.

2. Add prunes, celery, nuts, marshmallows and cherries. Turn into individual molds or shallow pan. Chill until firm.

3. Cut in 2½-ounce portions. Serve on lettuce. Garnish with cream mayonnaise.

GINGER PEACH MOLD

Yield: 48 molds

Ingredients

PEACHES, sliced	1½ No. 10 cans
GELATIN, ORANGE	1½ packages (36 ounces)
WATER, hot	2½ quarts
GINGERALE	2 quarts
PEACH JUICE	1 quart
SALT	½ teaspoon
ALMONDS, toasted, chopped	2 cups

Procedure

1. Drain peaches, reserving juice. Dissolve gelatin in hot water. Add gingerale, peach juice and salt. Cool and let congeal to egg white consistency. Add almonds and mix well. Cover bottom of mold with gelatin mixture. Lay 3 peach slices in mold. Finish filling mold with gelatin mixture. Chill until firm. Unmold; serve on lettuce leaf.

ALMOND-CREAM CAPPED SALAD MOLDS

Yield: 24 portions

Ingredients

ALMOND PASTE, creamy	1 cup
SOUR CREAM	2 cups
LEMON JUICE	2 tablespoons
ALMOND EXTRACT	1/4 teaspoon
GELATINE, unflavored	2 tablespoons
FRUIT SYRUP, DRAINED FROM CANNED PINEAPPLE, PEACHES or PEARS	1-1/3 cups
GELATIN, STRAWBERRY, LIME OR ORANGE FLAVOR, dissolved but not set	2-1/2 quarts
ICEBERG LETTUCE, half slices	24
STRAWBERRIES, hulled	24
ALMONDS, slivered	1/2 cup

Procedure

1. Crumble almond paste. Add sour cream, lemon juice and almond extract; beat until fairly smooth.

2. Soften unflavored gelatine in fruit syrup; stir over low heat until dissolved. Beat into almond paste mixture.

3. Turn about 3 tablespoons mixture into each of 24 individual molds. Chill until gently set.

4. Fill molds with prepared fruit flavored gelatin; chill until set.

5. Unmold onto halved slices of lettuce. Top with strawberry. Insert slivered almonds to complete garnish.

BING CHERRY SALAD

Yield: 48 ½-cup portions

Ingredients	
GELATINE, unflavored	2½ ounces
WATER, cold	1¼ quarts
BING CHERRIES, pitted, (in extra heavy syrup)	1 No. 10 can
CHERRY JUICE AND ORANGE JUICE to make	3 quarts
LEMON JUICE	1 cup
LEMON RIND, grated	2 teaspoons
SALT	2 teaspoons
SUGAR	1 cup
ALMOND EXTRACT	1 tablespoon

Procedure

1. Soften gelatine in cold water.

2. Drain cherries thoroughly. Measure syrup; add orange juice to make 3 quarts. Add lemon juice, lemon rind, salt, sugar and almond extract; stir until sugar is dissolved.

3. Dissolve gelatine over hot water; add to syrup mixture. Chill to unbeaten egg white consistency. Fold in drained cherries. Pour into individual molds or shallow pans. Chill until firm.

4. Unmold or cut in squares. Serve on crisp salad greens with sour cream dressing.

Note

May be served as a dessert with sweetened whipped cream or custard sauce.

JELLIED SHRIMP AND EGG SALAD

Yield: 50 ½-cup portions

Ingredients

GELATINE, unflavored	3 ounces
WATER, cold	2 cups
NONFAT DRY MILK	4 ounces
WATER	3-3/4 cups
HARD-COOKED EGGS, coarsely cut	24
SHRIMP, cooked, chopped	1 quart
GREEN PEPPER, chopped	1-1/2 cups
CELERY, finely cut	1-1/4 quarts
MAYONNAISE	1 quart
PIMENTOES, chopped	1-1/2 cups
PICKLE RELISH	1-1/8 cups
LEMON JUICE	1 cup

Procedure

1. Soak gelatine in first amount of water for 5 minutes.

2. Sprinkle nonfat dry milk on top of second amount of water; beat until smooth. Heat to boiling. Add softened gelatine; stir until dissolved. Chill until slightly thickened.

3. Fold remaining ingredients into gelatine mixture. Turn into individual molds or shallow pans. Chill until firm.

4. Unmold or cut into squares. Serve on crisp salad greens. Garnish with radishes, olives or sliced cucumbers.

TUNA MOUSSE

Yield: 2 gallons

Ingredients

GELATIN, LEMON	1½ pounds
WATER, hot	3½ quarts
LEMON JUICE	½ cup
VINEGAR	½ cup
CAYENNE	¼ teaspoon
WHIPPED TOPPING, prepared*	3 cups
MAYONNAISE	3 cups
TUNA, finely flaked	2½ pounds
CELERY, finely chopped	2 quarts
DILL PICKLES, chopped	1 cup
PIMIENTOES, chopped	½ cup

Procedure

1. Dissolve gelatin in hot water. Add lemon juice, vinegar and cayenne. Chill until slightly thickened.

2. Blend whipped topping and mayonnaise into gelatin mixture using a wire whip.

3. Mix in remaining ingredients.

4. Pour into shallow pans or large ring molds. Chill until firm.

5. Cut into portions. Serve on crisp salad greens. Garnish as desired.

*Prepare topping without sugar and vanilla.

TOMATO PECAN SALAD

Yield: 48 portions

Ingredients

GELATINE, unflavored	3½ ounces
WATER, cold	2 cups
TOMATO SOUP, canned	3 quarts
CREAM CHEESE, softened	1½ pounds
CHILI SAUCE	1 cup
MAYONNAISE	1 quart
CREAM, whipped*	1 quart
CELERY, chopped	1 quart
PECANS, chopped	1½ pounds

Procedure

1. Soften gelatine in cold water.

2. Heat soup over boiling water. Add softened gelatine; stir until completely dissolved.

3. Add softened cream cheese and chili sauce; blend. Chill until slightly thickened.

4. Fold in mayonnaise, whipped cream, celery and pecans.

5. Turn into two 12-inch by 20-inch by 2-inch pans. Chill until firm.

6. Cut into squares. Serve on crisp salad greens.

*Or, 1 quart whipped topping.

JELLIED RAW VEGETABLE SALAD

Yield: 1 gallon (32 ½-cup portions)

Ingredients

GELATINE, unflavored	6 tablespoons (1-1/2 ounces)
WATER, cold	2 cups
WATER, boiling	2 quarts
SUGAR	7/8 cup
SALT	2 tablespoons
VINEGAR	1 cup
ONION, minced	2 tablespoons
GREEN PEPPER, chopped	1/2 cup
CABBAGE, finely shredded	1 quart
CARROTS, raw, grated	1 quart

Procedure

1. Soften gelatine in cold water. Dissolve in boiling water. Add sugar; stir to dissolve. Chill until slightly thickened.

2. Combine salt, vinegar, onion, green pepper, cabbage and carrots. Let stand 10 to 15 minutes to marinate.

3. Fold vegetables into slightly thickened gelatine. Turn into individual molds or a 12-inch by 20-inch by 2-inch pan. Chill until firm.

4. Unmold or cut into squares. Serve on crisp salad greens.

MOLDED DATE WALDORF SALAD

Yield: 18 portions

Ingredients

GELATIN, LEMON	12 ounces
WATER, boiling	1 quart
ICE AND WATER	1 quart
LEMON JUICE	2 tablespoons
SUGAR	1 tablespoon
SALT	¼ teaspoon
APPLES, peeled	12 ounces
CELERY	12 ounces
DATES	4 ounces
MARASCHINO CHERRIES	1 ounce

Procedure

1. Dissolve gelatin in boiling water. Add ice and water; stir until ice is melted. Stir in lemon juice, sugar and salt.

2. Pour gelatin into 10-inch by 15-inch pan or two 10-inch by 3½-inch by 2½-inch loaf pans. Chill until slightly thickened.

3. Dice apples and celery into ¼-inch pieces. Chop dates and cherries.

4. Stir fruits and celery into gelatin. Chill until firm.

5. Cut pan 6 by 3 for 18 portions; cut loaf pans in 9. Serve portions on lettuce leaf.

SPRING DAY SALAD

Yield: 50 individual molds

Ingredients

GELATIN, LEMON	1½ pounds
	(3½ cups)
HOT WATER or PINEAPPLE JUICE, hot	2¾ quarts
CUCUMBERS, diced	2 cups
CELERY, finely diced	1 quart
PINEAPPLE, diced	3 cups
LEMON JUICE	1 cup
ALMONDS, blanched, coarsely chopped	2 cups
LETTUCE CUPS from	6 heads
MAYONNAISE	2 cups
SOUR CREAM	1 cup

Procedure

1. Dissolve gelatin in hot water or pineapple juice. Chill until slightly thickened.

2. Marinate cucumbers, celery and pineapple in the lemon juice.

3. Add marinated mixture and almonds to slightly thickened gelatin. Pour into individual molds; chill until firm.

4. Unmold; arrange in lettuce cup or on a bed of curly endive.

5. Blend mayonnaise and sour cream; use dressing to garnish salads.

JELLIED CHEESE SALAD

Yield: 25 portions

Ingredients

GELATINE, unflavored	¼ cup
WATER, cold	1½ cups
MILK, scalded	3 cups
ONION JUICE	2 tablespoons
SALT	1¼ teaspoons
CURRY POWDER	¾ teaspoon
DRY MUSTARD	¾ teaspoon
HOT PEPPER SAUCE	¼ teaspoon
PROCESS CHEESE, SHARP, shredded	3 pounds
HEAVY CREAM, whipped	1½ quarts
LETTUCE	as needed
TOMATO WEDGES	75
ARTICHOKE HEARTS	75
WATERCRESS	as needed

Procedure

1. Soften gelatine in cold water; dissolve in the scalded milk. Add onion juice, salt, curry powder, mustard and pepper sauce. Mix well. Cool.

2. Add cheese; blend together. Chill until slightly thickened. Fold in whipped cream; pour into individual molds. Chill until firm.

3. Unmold on crisp lettuce. Arrange tomato wedges and artichoke hearts around mold allowing three pieces of each per portion. Garnish with cress.

INDEX